EMMA-SUE PRINCE

THE ADVANTAGE

The 7 soft skills you need to stay one step ahead

PEARSON

Harlow, England • London • New York • Boston • San Francisco • Toronto • Sydney
Auckland • Singapore • Hong Kong • Tokyo • Seoul • Taipei • New Delhi
Cape Town • São Paulo • Mexico City • Madrid • Amsterdam • Munich • Paris • Milan

PEARSON EDUCATION LIMITED
Edinburgh Gate
Harlow CM20 2JE
United Kingdom
Tel: +44 (0)1279 623623
Web: www.pearson.com/uk

First published 2013 (print and electronic)

© Pearson Education Limited 2013 (print and electronic)

The right of Emma-Sue Prince to be identified as author of this work has been asserted
by her in accordance with the Copyright, Designs and Patents Act 1988.

Pearson Education is not responsible for the content of third-party internet sites.

ISBN: 978-1-4479-2956-7   (print)
       978-1-4479-2970-3   (PDF)
       978-1-4479-2971-0   (ePub)

British Library Cataloguing-in-Publication Data
A catalogue record for the print edition is available from the British Library

Library of Congress Cataloging-in-Publication Data
A catalog record for the print edition is available from the Library of Congress

10 9 8 7 6 5 4 3 2 1
17 16 15 14 13

Cover design by Dan Mogford
Cover image from iStockphoto
Print edition typeset in 10/14pt Plantin Std Regular by 30
Print edition printed and bound in Great Britain by Henry Ling Ltd, at the Dorset Press,
Dorchester, Dorset

NOTE THAT ANY PAGE CROSS REFERENCES REFER TO THE PRINT EDITION

This book is dedicated to my husband Nick, without whom writing it would not have been possible

Contents

About the author

Emma-Sue Prince has long specialised in soft skills, trainer training, materials design and management development. For many years she led an independent consultancy working with all of the above as well as becoming involved in new qualification design and business educational research, particularly within soft skills training. Her work has taken her all over the world and given her a leading reputation in the field.

She is the director of Unimenta, a training support network and virtual business focusing on supporting trainers who deliver soft skills by offering high quality materials, programme design, personalised support and professional development. Membership is free at www.unimenta.com.

Emma-Sue believes passionately in the principles and concepts she writes about in *The Advantage* and tries to apply them in all she does.

This is her first book.

www.the-advantage.info

Author's acknowledgements

The Advantage reflects contributions from various people along the way. In particular, I am very grateful to:

Nick English, my treasured husband, who patiently read draft after draft, gave me valuable suggestions, looked after our young son and gave up numerous weekends so I could write this text, and otherwise supports me in ways beyond expression.

Nicholas Bateson, dear friend and colleague, who helped with researching some of the psychological areas of the book. Nick is a career and executive coach, founder and director of London-based www.citycareercoach.com, specialises in coaching directors and senior leaders, and works regularly with several clients in the oil and gas industry, property management and investment banking.

Jon Wilkerson, dear friend and colleague, who has inspired me to use the principles of comedy improvisational theatre in my personal and professional life and who has supported me throughout the writing of this text. Based in Denver, Colorado, USA, Jon Wilkerson, director of www.internationalfunny business.com has taught thousands of people how to be more effective in their personal and professional lives by mastering the principles of improvisation

Eloise Cook, who has been a wonderful editor and support throughout, providing insightful suggestions and ideas.

Publisher's acknowledgements

We are grateful to the following for permission to reproduce copyright material:

Stop and Think! text on page 21 from 'The nightmare scenario,' *The Economist*, 19/05/2012 (Bagehot).

In some instances we have been unable to trace the owners of copyright material, and we would appreciate any information that would enable us to do so.

Foreword

Emma-Sue has been on the road of self-understanding and awareness for many years. I have known her as a client and colleague for most of that time. *The Advantage* brings together all of the common sense she has, knowledge that she has accumulated, from both her professional and home life and the sensitivity of someone with real emotional intelligence, without any of the dogma one might fear.

As a psychotherapist and counsellor for 28 years, I try to help people step back and be able to look at themselves more objectively. This can lead ultimately to making real choices whilst accepting that there are some things that can't be changed. As one client put it, 'Becoming more of an expert on yourself'.

Each chapter in this text is original and unique, focusing on inner resources and skills that each of us has, if we genuinely want to develop them. *The Advantage* is pragmatic and helps you feel in control of your life, be better able to achieve your ambitions, without controlling or being controlled. It does away with the regret of the past and fear of the future which prevents us from living in, and making the best of, the present.

The worst place to be is feeling stuck, trapped and helpless. This text will help you never be in that place. 'You could do better' does not mean that 'you should just try harder'. We can't control what or how we feel. Managing your feelings does not mean indulging them, though.

Each chapter helps you look at fundamental concepts in an original and personal way which, if explored and embraced, must make it better than it would have been otherwise. And give a real advantage.

Dr Malcolm Kirsh
The Hale Clinic, London

Introduction

I have written *The Advantage* because I know that each of the seven skills I describe have contributed to the success of my own life, but I only really became aware of this through writing the text. Being adaptable will make the difference between being ordinary and extraordinary. The right critical thinking skills enable you to be creative, resourceful and smart. Without empathy, how can you have a healthy, clear and meaningful relationship, not only with yourself but with others too? You need integrity to live a life aligned to values and accountability. Without healthy optimism, it's difficult to create the life you want to lead. If you're proactive, grab opportunities and understand how to respond to what's around you, rather than react, you will succeed. And to do all of this requires resilience and strength.

> without healthy optimism, it's difficult to create the life you want to lead

My life experiences have not been easy, but I know my life is and has been rich, exciting, wonderful and challenging, and will continue to be. From a young age I had to learn to be self-reliant, adopting a survivor attitude for coping with mental health issues in my family, major moves to Germany and the USA with a lot of disruption to my schooling, sexual abuse and leaving home at 16 with no family support. This led to several years of difficulty in my late teens and early twenties, which included single parenting, divorce, severe financial hardship and the loss of my mother to a violent road accident.

By the age of 25 I had been through what most people experience in twice that time. It took me a long time to confront and handle the subsequent emotions, blame and bad relationship decisions I made. It took me even longer to embrace my experiences and make them part of who I am today.

Whether I am adaptable and resilient naturally, or as a result of my early life experiences, I have certainly never shied away from taking on challenges and I was always determined to make the very best of things. I didn't want to struggle financially, so I made sure I got the education I needed and it turned out I was good at making money. I've had to be proactive in creating a life that made sense for me and didn't mean being stuck in a rut. Getting the education I had missed was so important to me that my early career included working in a cheese shop, coffeehouse, bakery and several restaurants and bars, often working two or sometimes three jobs to make ends meet.

Throughout my life, I've always been optimistic – it's been tough but I've made it happen. Critical thinking helped me to be creative and resourceful when it came to working out what I needed in order to be where I wanted to be.

I've been through the whole self-help movement, reading dozens of books and doing hundreds of different exercises. Some helped, some didn't. What really helped through some of the most difficult times was a hard-nosed therapist who urged me to get up and make the most of my life, skills and potential. To even begin to do that I had to build empathy skills and integrity – both had to start with ME. Hard work? Yes, but worth it.

Such therapists and counsellors are very rare. However, *The Advantage* gives you a shortcut to some of the lessons I learned.

So where have the skills led me? Career-wise my work evolved over the years and has included teaching, lecturing, training, research, qualification design, building my own consultancy business, designing training programmes, supporting disadvantaged young people, volunteering, serving on charity boards and being a trustee. All of this has involved creativity, taking risks and recognising and grabbing opportunities. My work has enabled me to travel widely to countries where there is extraordinary poverty and social issues, for which insight I am extremely grateful. I'm passionate about training, improving skills and developing people.

I am now happily married to the love of my life, with a young family. I live in a wonderful community of which I am an active member. I have fantastic work–life balance. Life is good. But it always has been, really. And now I have written this text.

We each have our own stories and our own experiences. We each can develop and become the very best of ourselves. I'm still working on it.

I know from my own experiences that these seven skills can and do make the difference and give any of us an advantage in our lives. I want you to experience this too.

So why not you, why not now?

'Everyone thinks of changing the world,
but no one thinks of changing himself.'

Leo Tolstoy

THE WORLD WE ARE LIVING IN

Have you noticed how the world has altered incredibly in recent years? We are living in times of unprecedented change, complexity and competition. Advances in technology, globalisation, economic uncertainty, the shifting workplace and changing social dynamics are presenting us all with challenges and opportunities never before experienced. And everything happens so fast.

Coupled with this, it's becoming plain that schools, universities and employers are not equipping us with the tools and skills we need to prosper in today's world. We learn information and how to do things, but we all seem to be working harder and longer without seeing any real benefit. According to many in the West over the last ten years, we could not have worked harder, we had to borrow money, we had to buy property, that new car and go on that expensive holiday. And now we can't work any harder, we can't start businesses because banks won't lend us money, we can't find a job because there aren't any/we are too old/don't have enough experience and we can't leave the country to work or live elsewhere. Something has to give, because it's just not working the way things are at the moment.

So what will give us the advantage to be truly effective in our lives? And not just in the workplace, but also at home and with our loved ones?

The answer can be found in the soft skills, or people skills and the character traits that underpin successful and effective people. These people aren't just good at being an effective team player or a good leader or communicating persuasively – they have a whole host of skills at their fingertips. You may or may not be familiar with soft skills, and the term can be interpreted in many different ways. For example, hard skills are tangibles such as writing a business plan or preparing a budget. They are usually associated with technical knowledge and understanding of a process. Another example: employability skills might focus on the mechanics of applying for a job, such as writing a good CV, but the soft skills would be how well you present at interview and your ability to be self-confident.

This text redefines soft skills as the 'personal competencies' that really make a difference, that will help each and every one of us cope better with extraordinary change and challenges, grab the opportunities that are coming and live better and happier lives as a result.

Each of us now needs to develop stronger personal skills that help us to work well, reach our potential, be financially secure, have a fulfilling relationship and family life and, basically, contribute to society and life with the best of ourselves that we have to offer. We each need to step up to the table and take on personal responsibility for developing the competences and skills we need not only to survive in the world we now live in, but to thrive in it.

it's time to take responsibility for our own futures

The good news is that we can all develop these essential skills – seven in all. *The Advantage* shows you why these skills will be more important, now and in the future, than ever before and why it's so important to develop them. More importantly still, it will show you how to develop these skills, how to use and apply them and be truly successful and effective as a result.

So, who's to blame?

Dissatisfaction has erupted and we've developed a blame culture, as you will notice if you read widely on the whole subject of the economic crisis. There is blaming of government, the bankers, the companies that reorganise and downsize, or the world decision makers, and far less emphasis on individuals taking responsibility and actually dealing with the new reality.

But blaming the politicians and bankers for the current crisis in the West is narrow-minded and unhelpful. Whatever the circumstance we find ourselves in, we are not helpless victims – each of us has untapped potential and strengths that most are not using to the full. What better way to discover these than a situation that challenges you like never before? Another way of looking at the times we now live in is to view them as an exciting era of opportunity and change. Difficult and challenging – yes. Impossible to rise above and succeed? Not necessarily, especially if you look from within for your strength, resource and security.

The fact is that there is a lot of gloom and doom out there. In his book *Global Trends*, Adrian Done says that, essentially, we're living in a world with a highly uncertain economic outlook and with living conditions worsening for millions because of past failures and not dealing with what was 'foreseeable and actionable'. But shouldn't we look at this as an opportunity for each of us to rise up to the challenge, to actually take responsibility, to become and be the very best of ourselves? We need to start relying more on ourselves and on our inner resources.

In the past we didn't need to be **resilient** or **optimistic** – two key personal competences we need to have now. We didn't need to be self-contained because we were too busy riding the wave, spending money we didn't have and relying on a seemingly secure and supportive external environment with easy credit, secure jobs, and so on.

Our education and experience is not equipping us with the tools and skills we need and this has become more apparent during the economic crisis. It's time for change!

New skills for the world we now live in

The idea of personal competences and employability skills is nothing new. It was established well over ten years ago that people entering the workforce lacked skills such as oral communication, collaboration, work ethic, self-discipline, written communication and problem solving; these have loosely become known as 'twenty-first-century skills'.[1] But even with such skills firmly on the agenda, it seems things are getting no better. They are still lacking across all levels of the workplace, from the top to the bottom. So why is this?

In the past ten years, society, the way we interact and communicate with each other and, more recently, the dramatic economic events have, quite simply, made these skills less relevant and urgent. This is partly because skills such as written communication and problem solving are hugely impacted by the fast rise in use of various technologies, and partly because the good economic times we experienced before the downturn meant we didn't really have to worry about them because the glass was always half full.

Of course these skills are still vitally important, but it is becoming harder to develop them without the inner resources required. And, perhaps surprisingly, as I will explain later, new technology and how we use that technology to communicate still requires strong interpersonal skills. They are the key to success in the modern workplace and so these trends are deeply concerning. We have not been strengthening our ability to focus, communicate and collaborate and we are now weakening this ability significantly, each and every day. We need to slow down. Speed, whether because of fast thinking and actions or technology, is making us bad communicators – we listen poorly to others and figure out where they are headed after the first few words and then interrupt. Executive function means to focus, ignore distractions, remember and use new information, action planning, revising the plan and inhibiting fast impulsive thoughts and actions. **Empathy** will be a key skill to harness and develop for all our relationships, whether off- or online.

these skills can make THE difference

What's driving these trends?

So, let's take a closer look at some of the most important trends and changes in the world we live in and what those, in turn, mean for the seven key personal competences and skills we now need to develop.

Technology

Advances in technology have completely transformed the world we are living in. We live in a big, fat, connected world – we are online more and more and globalisation means we are competing, not just locally, but internationally too.

Technology is a key factor behind why our soft/interpersonal skills are in need of help. Why? There are two reasons, which are closely related:

1 We now spend an increasing amount of time interacting with an electronic screen, as well as being bombarded with a sheer overload of information, messages and data. This means that interpersonal skills, which are best developed face to face and through experimentation and repetition, are being ignored.

2 All this time spent 'online' impacts our ability to focus attention, concentrate and listen – key elements of effective communication. Just think of a typical evening at home, 'relaxing': chances are you're probably watching a film while chatting to someone, checking something on the Internet,

answering email and texting. You think you're multi-tasking, but your brain is actually becoming less able to focus efficiently. What you are really doing is simply shifting from one task to the other and dividing your attention.

Stop and think!

I experienced this recently when I caught myself in the bad habit of taking my iPad to bed, planning to read my latest book download. However, despite telling myself not to, I got distracted and ended up checking email, Twitter and Facebook. This didn't help me to relax, so my sleep was disrupted. It was a very easy habit to fall into, and much harder to break.

In terms of the technology itself, products are developed and become outdated far more quickly than before. Technical, detailed knowledge of, say, an iPad is obsolete in less than three years compared with, for example, a car of the 1950s. Back then an engineer could repair engines successfully over decades with the same knowledge. Today, we have to work much harder to keep ahead of changes.

There is now a massive rate of Internet use. We use blogs, wikis, websites and social media as daily communication tools, whether as individuals, professionals or businesses. There is an explosion in social networking sites and micro blogging through Twitter.

If you think things have changed beyond all recognition in the last twenty, ten or even five years in terms of technology and social media, this will only increase. There'll be further incremental changes of existing technologies – how would wireless energy transfer Avatar-style robotics or anti-ageing drugs impact *your* life, for example? Technology familiar to us now will continue to evolve and change further. For example, I have a discussion forum on my website but I can already see that, in only a short space of time, this is becoming an outdated way of sharing information and discussions, given the explosion of Twitter and social media. So don't try harder with stuff you are already familiar with – you need to embrace the new and keep moving and learning. Generally, these changes will be incremental so you hardly notice them. This makes it even more important to make sure your efforts are constant and part of your daily life. It's not going to be enough to say to yourself, 'I think I'll learn something new today'. It's dangerous to ignore the potential for further development. Things are changing every day!

> your soft skills become even more important with each new technological advance

There is also a flip side – many companies go under as result of not being able to adapt to new ways of doing things, but statistics show that even more new companies are created through innovation and the ability to innovate quickly. Technology can open up lots of new opportunities to new players with the right focus and determination.

A good example of how the necessary competences needed in a particular sector are changing is the advent of 3D printing. 3D printing can now create a single item as cheaply as mass-producing thousands. Prototypes can be made quickly and cheaply. Right now it is difficult to predict the long-term impact of 3D printing, but economists say it will impact the world as profoundly as the factory once did. Therefore, it makes sense that those businesses or individuals that grab and act on opportunities within the 3D printing sector will likely thrive, though they will take some risks to do so.

Societies, businesses and individuals open-minded enough to embrace such technology are certainly more likely to flourish because it's now easier and cheaper to produce new prototypes and get new products to market. This is a further reason to become more adaptable, as you need this skill to cope with all of these changes. You must be able to think the unthinkable and thrive in spite of it. **Adaptability** is a key competence in today's world.

Some of this may seem scary and daunting at first and calls upon us to embrace change and move forward with confidence, determination and optimism – all qualities we have inside ourselves and a vital resource now.

The workplace

This is constantly evolving and changing. Traditional organisational structures have been fading for some time, and even the 'office', our place of work, is changing. Our tools and technologies shape the kinds of social, economic and political organisations we inhabit. These changes will mean that we need to rise to the following challenges:

- Being more in control of our work and careers. Job security doesn't really exist any more in the way we like to think of it. The CEO and founder of LinkedIn, Reid Hoffman, says in his book *The Start-up of You* that we are natural entrepreneurs and it is the entrepreneurial way of thinking that will help us in this new era. We need to rediscover these instincts. He speaks of work and career being a predictable 'escalator' – of following a specific path of education, work experience, training, job and promotions. Now this escalator is 'jammed' at every point. We need to, and have to, find ways to 'unjam' this escalator. Being **proactive**, another key skill, will take on a whole new meaning.

- Working flexibly, smartly and autonomously, collaborating virtually across different time zones and geographies. Our face-to-face interpersonal skills need to be replicated in how we communicate virtually over the Internet and email, and cross-culturally. That's where **empathy** comes in.

- Becoming far better and more efficient at working with data. Whether running a business or managing our individual health and finances, our work and personal lives will increasingly demand abilities to interact with data, see patterns in data, make data-based decisions and use data to design desired outcomes. New media technologies are bringing about a transformation in the way we communicate. This will require us to really step up our **critical thinking skills** as we know them.

● We'll be working way past retirement age so it's important that you are doing work that you enjoy, that you are skilled at and that enables you to keep reinventing yourself. There are many exciting opportunities, but they also mean shedding our traditional view of work and career as we think of them now.

> changes in the workplace mean opportunities for work–life balance, new business and working to your strengths

Everything in the workplace is now performance-based and short-term, so all the rules have changed. No job is secure. So people need new skills for the new economy! We need to be adapting all the time and we'll stay young and agile by doing so.

Globalisation

The West no longer holds a monopoly on job creation, innovation and political power. The economic and political orbit has tilted towards the BRIC countries (Brazil, Russia, India and China) and it's a trend that shows no sign of stopping, despite economic dips. We're all familiar with the example of the call centre in India. Outsourcing like this has led to loss of jobs in IT, customer service and software development in the West, but this isn't the end of the BRIC countries' development. Emerging markets are now also climbing the social scale – going beyond poaching low-paid manufacturing jobs towards higher-end research and development roles, innovation and design. India has 200 million graduates, and

UK and US universities are capitalising on this by expanding overseas. The University of Lancashire has just opened its first UK campus in Thailand at an investment of £7.5m, with many more providing TNE (trans-national education) in Malaysia, China and Singapore.[2] India has set up 14 research and innovation-themed universities in collaboration with US institutions. This is significant as, in the UK anyway, the higher education market is considered to be only at the beginning of globalisation.[3]

Thus, competition for jobs will be ever more ferocious in the globalised marketplace. Jobs will be increasingly polarised between well-paid, highly technical and professional jobs and service-type jobs in retail, leisure, health and hospitality, which are poorly paid. However, this globalisation will also create opportunities for diverse cultures to work with each other, and individuals with this capacity will be at a competitive advantage.[4]

The BRIC economies are growing *fast* and with this comes political power.[5] If you're not involved with these countries in some way, you are likely to be in an ever-shrinking pond, so here is yet another reason to up your skills! Despite recent economic turmoil and social changes, China, India, Russia and Brazil will still continue to be huge potential powerhouses that drive world economy. The USA is the world's biggest debtor and China its largest creditor. If current trends persist, China will be the world's second largest economy by 2025.

you need to take initiative, be flexible, and why not learn another foreign language?

There are lots of opportunities within our changing geopolitical landscape – medium-sized rising powers such as Brazil, Indonesia and Turkey will be able to redefine their roles regionally and internationally, creating new forums to resolve geopolitical issues. There will be a greater need for collaboration within business and society.

Within such a changing and dynamic geopolitical landscape, individuals who are well informed, prepared to be flexible in the face of change and prepared to adapt will have the best chance to prosper. It will open up space for new entrepreneurs to address market needs across the globe. In developed nations this can maintain the current standard of living, and in emerging nations can lift people out of poverty.[6] It also means that people will become more mobile and be more open to working and living in different countries.

Demographic changes

The current demographic changes we are experiencing are going to have a significant impact on how we live and work. We are living longer, are generally healthier and we are also expected to work for longer. Retiring on full pension at age 65 or younger is already a thing of the past for the majority and, in the future, working until you are into your seventies and even eighties will not be unusual. Increasing global lifespans mean that young people will face competition from more skilled and experienced older people. At current trends worldwide, there will be only four potential workers per each 65+-year-old by 2050.[7] What this means is that if we were to continue to expect to retire at around the age of 65, there wouldn't be any sustainable form of financial support. This is something we need to accept. It is a sobering fact that means we simply have no alternative but to adapt and embrace the new future that is here now.

Young people everywhere need to develop these skills too, to grab opportunities and build new businesses. And, surely also, the old can work with the young? We may see a big comeback of mentoring. I also think it is important generally to encourage those elderly, wherever they are, to be willing to make valuable contributions to business, economy and society beyond traditional retirement threshold.

Businesses that manage to retain the experience and valuable knowledge of a senior workforce, while at the same time capturing the vitality of a young diverse workforce, will be the ones who excel in this scenario.

Stop and think!

Think this is a bitter pill to swallow? Get over it – you could be working till you are much older so you had better be doing something that you really love and that plays to your strengths. All the more incentive for you to increase your personal skills and competencies and look inward for the resources that you will need to cope. And each of us has the resources to cope. We all have far more capacity than we think to be resilient, proactive and adaptable!

Personally, I have no expectation of retiring because I see my work as bound up intrinsically with my strengths and what I contribute to the world. Indeed, I see my work in phases of reinventing myself, drawing on all the experience and skills I've gained over the years and becoming better and better at what I do. People in mid-life career need to keep being innovative, changing in readiness for the next part of their career, not only because of working longer but also because the way they work or where they work might change. What you've been doing for the last ten years or so may not sustain the next part of your career. Individually, we need to keep an open mind on our expectations in later life. We're all in for a longer life anyway, so we need to find ways of making this healthy, contented and fulfilling rather than the opposite, or anticipating the opposite.

The best opportunities will be for the well educated who can make a valuable contribution to society and business. They'll be in constant demand everywhere. Emerging and developing economies will provide entrepreneurial activities, career development and personal growth for value-adders.

Health

We know we are going to live for longer. Living longer is not necessarily great if those extra years are spent suffering from poor health. It is much more important to live longer lives in *better* states of health. Part of developing personal competences and skills is an increasing awareness and responsibility for our own health. And it's proven that, if you are stronger physically, you are more likely to be resilient mentally too.

Resilience is another key skill we have to have. The nature of our health problems is changing unexpectedly as a combined result of global ageing, urbanisation, globalised lifestyle changes, accelerated worldwide transmission of communicable diseases and the higher burden of chronic disorders. In high-income countries, 70 per cent of all deaths are among people over 70 and this elderly population are more likely to suffer from multiple chronic conditions as they get older. In the West, we are likely to see a return to younger members of the family increasingly caring for the elderly, as the healthcare system will not be able to support the level of care required and the costs of such care are likely to rise.

Our health and our lifestyles are linked to our inner resources and skills. For example, it is proven that if you want to build psychological resilience, starting with the body and building physical strength can drive this forward significantly. If we develop our ability to be **optimistic**, it is well known that those with optimism live longer and more healthily. And we also need optimism to face our lives and our futures with determination and vigour.

Many of the skills we need to strengthen have their roots in neuroscience and our brains. For example, it is now proven that we can develop what's known as our 'working memory', and that this actually gets stronger with age. Why is this important? Our working memory is like a mental jotting pad that enables us to adapt and change our behaviour. Knowing that this improves with age, as opposed to declining (as traditionally thought) is a breakthrough and turns our view of ageing on its head.

Likewise, strengthening the body through Yoga, Pilates, exercise and meditation has a strong impact on our mental capacity and is linked with our ability to demonstrate **empathy**, another key competence and one that we are hard-wired to have. Strengthening our bodies in this way has a positive effect on our ability to be resilient.

> meditation, yoga and pilates are becoming more and more popular as ways to help build resilience and empathy skills

Education

In the West we are overeducating without providing essential skills. Our young people are finishing education without the skills they need to be employable. The number of young people leaving school and college with serious shortfalls in their employability skills is still high, according to the CBI/EDI Education and Skills Survey 2012.[8] The top weaknesses in both school-leavers and graduates alike are communication, team working, problem solving and self-management. This is also reflected in global surveys too. There is a widespread weakness in core workplace skills among existing employees, with literacy and numeracy topping the list. Around 775 million adults worldwide can't read or manage a bank account – that is 16 per cent of the global population, including the West.

Students in developed countries are simply being stuffed with too many complex things, given where their lives are likely to go. They tend to be 'overqualified' and, these days, a university degree does not guarantee you a job nor does it equip you with employability and essential soft skills. A further issue is that economic pressures to work are pushing younger and younger children into full-time daycare or nursery education, which in turn produces an overload of 'learning'. Generally, education in the West and in emerging markets now starts too young and goes on for too long. Education systems are not aligned to the labour market so there is the potential of steady and systemic unemployment. Even if jobs are available, individuals without appropriate training are unlikely to possess the required skill set. Governments need to engage with businesses more to determine what they really want and need and these requirements need to be included in education. This is starting to happen but there is a long way to go.

Again, the blame culture in the West puts the onus on teachers, schools, classroom size, funding, government and parents rather than placing any responsibility onto young people themselves. However, this approach allows it to be OK for individuals not to be responsible for their actions because the root cause of failure to achieve is believed to lie not in an individual but in the situation or external factors. This, in turn, echoes back to how we have been responding to world events and economic changes. The good news is that it is possible for young people to develop these skills without an expensive education or training, or necessarily waiting until they are employed.

each of us is capable of developing these skills

Generally, having young people study and specialise through university is a good thing as long as they can put this into practice; it needs to be for a purpose, otherwise a degree in a humanity is a luxury few can afford unless they intend to go into further training such as accountancy, teaching or law. However, even these professions are now fast-tracking undergraduates and school-leavers with good results, without necessarily demanding a degree first. Graduates who are generalists can no longer automatically step into a well-paid job. In Germany, for example, young people can learn one of 350 skilled trades through their vocational schools. Teenagers not bound for university apply for three-year programmes combining classroom learning with practical experience within companies, which have fully bought into the scheme. A massive two-thirds of schoolchildren in Germany undertake apprenticeships, and the cost is shared between the company and the government and generally positively regarded in German society. The result is superior German quality in everything, from haircuts to waitressing! Of course, there has been wide criticism of this system and Germany has been accused of not producing enough graduates, but in our current economy isn't this dual system starting to look more attractive?[9] In the UK, vocational training has long been seen as less attractive because of a belief that it is somehow second-best to an academic education. More recently, Germany has brought their apprenticeship model to the USA via Volkswagen and, next year, its first class of US apprentices will complete their training.[10] These sorts of programmes are gaining in popularity and will likely continue to do so.

There is an absolutely clear need for lifelong learning. Our modern world is complex and it certainly does not allow for any stagnation of thinking once you have a degree. There is always more knowledge to be gained. Martin Seligman, in his book *Flourish*, says that all young people need to learn both workplace skills and the skills of wellbeing and positive psychology. He says that if you were to ask parents what they want for their children they would probably tell you that they want their children to be happy, confident, balanced, kind, healthy and loving. Schools teach achievement, thinking skills, success, literacy, test-taking and discipline. Seligman argues that what is important is to build character strengths such as honesty, loyalty, perseverance, creativity, kindness, wisdom, courage and fairness as well.

We now need appropriate and useful theoretical knowledge, together with practical skills, social values and employability skills. The teaching of values, lifelong skills, literacy and numeracy will remain essential to equip future generations.

Making it happen

Much of traditional self-help says that if you want to improve your life, you first have to change how you think through positive visualisation and affirmations, as well as just generally thinking positively. This will, in turn, have an impact on your emotions and how you feel, following which, your behaviour and outcomes will change. In principle, some of this sounds perfectly reasonable, but in practice, these methods are often ineffective. One reason could be to do with the fact that affirmation and visualisation is achieved through using relaxation techniques and that none of these gives any focus to dealing with the setbacks, sheer effort and hard work that go with striving towards any goal or behaviour change.

Yet change IS possible. Decades of research shows that there is indeed a simple but highly effective way to transform how you think and feel through focusing first on how you are behaving.[11] By using and applying the seven soft skills outlined in this text, you will start to tap into and develop your inner resources that enable you to do this.

The Economist magazine, May 2012, featured a 1956 short story by Julio Cortazar.[12] The story is about a young man injured in a motorcycle accident, lying in hospital, who is tormented by vivid and recurring nightmares about being hunted by Aztec warriors. *The Economist* writer likens the young man's experience with how many Europeans are feeling – yearning to hear that austerity, cuts and hardship are, in fact, just a nightmare from which they will awaken.

Stop and think!

Cortazar's story ends with a twist: the man realises that he is, in reality, an Aztec prisoner. Modern life, the hospital, his motorcycle like 'an enormous metal insect whirring away between his legs' was the absurd dream, falling away as he awaits death. Britons and other Europeans need to go through a similarly vertiginous moment. For decades, workers faced with exploding global competition, early retirement and welfare on credit dreamed of affluence for life to replace jobs for life. Now the competition is as intense as ever, societies are ageing and their nations are poorer than they ever thought only a few years ago. The boom years were the dream. Hard work and tighter belts are the new reality![13]

In the same sense as the story, we too have been living a dream and not doing what we needed to do. So we are now having to make up for lost time, and fast, against a very challenging and moving background of uncertainty. We all do have within us what we need to succeed in the new world, but over the last 20 years or so we've not developed as a society and as individuals, we have become dormant. It is, indeed, as if we have been sleep-walking and now it's time to wake up.

So what's this all about?

With such changes going on, it's clear that we have no option but to rise to the challenges around us. We have a real opportunity now, more than ever before, to become 'better versions' of ourselves and truly reach our full potential. And we can. Each of us really does possess the resources and capability within to develop the key personal skills and competences that we need. We need to think about all of these challenges and be proactive in thinking about how we are going to respond to them. Each day presents an opportunity to learn more, do more, be more, grow more.

We are entering a new era. We CAN do more with less. Eighty per cent of effects come from twenty per cent of causes. It's important to focus on the small things you can do and not to be overwhelmed by the thought of having to suddenly develop a whole set of new skills. Trying to work on everything at the same time wastes effort and resources and progress is limited. Taking small steps and acting on that most important 20 per cent is what will make the difference.

So what are the personal competences that will give you the ADVANTAGE? There are seven skills that are going to help you succeed, get or create that job, find your true strengths and fulfil your potential.

Here they are:

1   **Adaptability:** It's more important than ever to be flexible, adaptable and agile, with plenty of resourcefulness and creativity to help you respond effectively to challenges and grab new opportunities. Why? Because things now change at a far greater speed and pace than ever before. Change is with us and it's constant.

2   **Critical thinking:** Your attitude needs to be more open than ever. Critical thinking is raw material for twenty-first century success! To challenge assumptions, we have to be able to look at things from different angles, think outside the box, collaborate with others, clarify goals and find solutions. Problem-solving skills have never been so crucial. You must be brave enough to challenge conventional approaches and be adaptable to changing situations and circumstances. Experiment when you can, otherwise, once your old ways have ceased to be effective, you'll be stuck.

3   **Empathy:** This is the ability and capacity to really understand what someone else is experiencing and to walk a mile in their shoes. Why is empathy important? Because without it you will never have strong listening skills or the ability to respect others and really value your relationships. Everything you do is now more visible than ever. Managing and nurturing all your relationships well is a key skill and competence.

4   **Integrity:** As the speed of life has accelerated, so has the number of people who are neglecting to do the things that are expected of them, such as being on time for appointments, returning calls, and completing projects on time. These may seem like small things but they are not! Trust, values, principles and honesty are the name of the game now, as is authenticity. You must consistently behave in ways that are in line with your values. Throughout periods of intense change, be consistent – a harbour in the storm.

5   **Optimism:** Get used to being disappointed and rejected! Know how to develop and keep a positive attitude, no matter

what life throws at you. But even that is not enough – you need to generate and radiate good will and positive energy to maintain a competitive edge. You need to be the most positive person you know! In the absence of certainty, you need to be able to influence and inspire others around you.

6 **Proactivity:** You probably will have to reinvent yourself a number of times throughout your life and work. Being proactive means thinking and acting ahead and using foresight. These days, more than ever before, employers are looking for self-starters, not someone who needs to have their hand held. You are more likely to end up working for yourself, having a portfolio career or starting your own business. At the very least you'll be changing jobs and roles a number of times.

7 **Resilience:** Dealing with ambiguity, coping with stress and overcoming set-backs can be emotionally draining, psychologically demanding and intellectually challenging. Resilience helps you to bounce back and respond at your best. To quote Rudyard Kipling, 'If you can keep your head when all about you are losing theirs and blaming it on you; if you can trust yourself when all men doubt you, but make allowance for their doubting too,' then 'yours is the earth'.

So, how do we develop and maintain these key skills? A simple formula: achievement = skills × effort. A person contributes their 'effort' to the equation and effort is the amount of time spent on a task. The cornerstone of all high expertise is not God-given genius but deliberate practice and the amount of time and energy spent in dedicated practice. Mozart was Mozart not primarily because he had a unique gift but mainly because from toddlerhood he did nothing but use his gift. If you want to become world-class at anything you must spend 60 hours a week on it for 10 years! I am not suggesting here that we all do this to perfect our skills and competences, but the principle here is about working on developing these skills and behaviours, consistently and steadily. Hard and thoughtful work is required.

So, now you know what you need and why you need it. With these skills you will have the capacity and ability to thrive. I suppose the key question is how we develop these skills and competences? Why do some people find some easier to manifest than others? Can they be learned? Read on to find out more.

Each section in *The Advantage* deals with one of these skills. It looks at what the skill is and why we need it in our changing world and why it's important. Each skill can be developed in different ways and it's about understanding how much of that is down to your own character and personality and how much is related to life circumstances. The focus is on giving you the key facts and latest research and some straightforward ways for you to develop these skills. Each section ends with 10 ways to develop the skill and a 'day in the life of' case study that takes you through someone's day, holding up a magnifying glass to that skill and how it makes a difference.

If you then want to take more time to focus on these skills, you can visit www.the-advantage.info where you will find online tips, exercises and ideas for incorporating these skills on a day-to-day basis. If you are a trainer or facilitator, do visit our support site for anyone delivering soft skills, at www.unimenta.com. Membership is free.

Interested in reading more?

Done, A. (2012) *Global Trends, Facing up to a Changing World.* Palgrave Macmillan

Gladwell, M. (2009) *Outliers: The Story of Success.* Penguin

Hoffman, R. and Casnocha, B. (2012) *The Start-up of You: Adapt to the Future, Invest in Yourself, and Transform Your Career.* Random House Business Books

Seligman, M. (2011) *Flourish, A New Understanding of Happiness and Wellbeing and How to Achieve Them.* Heinemann

'It is not the strongest of the species that survives, nor the most intelligent that survives. It is the one that is the most adaptable to change.'

Charles Darwin

Chapter 1

ADAPTABILITY

A daptability is an attractive quality. We all like to think of ourselves as being flexible and adaptable. It means that we are not rigid or stuck and so are open to change and challenge. I think if you were to ask most people if they consider themselves to be open and adaptable, they would tell you 'yes'.

What is adaptability?

Adaptability can be defined as the ability to change (or be changed) to fit altered circumstances. Every one of us has the basic capability to be adaptable; without this being hard-wired in us we would not be able to function in the world. Throughout our lives we adapt, and indeed have to. We adapt to school, to new environments, to work, to relationships, to learning and developing. Even though it is natural to resist change because we don't want to let go, our capacity to adapt is probably greater than we think. That's because it's a basic survival skill – the ability to adapt smarter or faster than any current situation is what has allowed humans to flourish and consistently make progress since caveman days.

Adaptability is more than being flexible, though – it is about being open to things, even outside our comfort zone, and not stating pre-conceived judgements such as 'I could never do that' or 'That will be too hard for me'. It's about developing more of what we are truly capable of and living up to our potential. And we may well talk ourselves out of that more than we think we do.

Change is difficult because we want to stay inside our comfort zone and will resist anything that requires us to step out of it. Therefore, a conscious effort is needed to do this for those of us less open to change, and even for those of us who are. Our comfort zones are, basically, as small or as big as we make them. We make them bigger by engaging in more activities, tasks, thoughts and experiences that lie outside of our comfort zone. And the bigger our comfort zone, the more adaptable we will be!

> your comfort zone is the key to how adaptable you are. Make it bigger and your ability to adapt soars

Adaptability enables us continually to work towards and fulfil our individual potential and to not necessarily stop once we've reached a certain level or point in our career and life. This is probably a good thing, given that we are all going to be living and working for longer.

Surely the more opportunities there are (or that we are presented with) that invite us to adapt successfully, the better! Doesn't this mean embracing change rather than our natural first reaction, which is to resist it? Adaptability in our world today means a whole bunch of things:

- keeping calm in the face of difficulties
- embracing uncertainty
- persisting in the face of difficulties
- taking on new challenges at short notice
- saying 'YES' to challenges
- dealing with changing priorities and workloads
- improvising
- bouncing back from setbacks and showing a positive attitude
- keeping an open mind
- seeing the bigger picture
- coping well with the unexpected.

Adaptability is all of these, and more.

When we push the envelope, when we intentionally put ourselves in situations that are outside our comfort zone, there is no doubt that we grow. Being adaptable can lead to tangible results in our work but can also make us feel much happier as we discover what we are truly capable of being or doing and as we fulfil more and more of our human potential.

Why is adaptability so important?

We know it's now more important than ever to be flexible and agile, with plenty of resourcefulness and creativity to respond effectively to challenges and grab new opportunities. Why? Because things now change at a far greater speed and pace than ever before. Change is with us, it seems constant and, as we have seen in recent years, so are disappointment and difficult times. The ability to bounce back, reassess and adapt is a top one. Yet, when change is imposed from the outside, such as our recent economic situation and crisis, this creates stress which means we can actually become less adaptable and flexible and start to exhibit behaviours that are counter-productive to achieving results. According to Ken Buch, Senior Consultant with Managing Concepts Inc., people in the midst of change tend to experience heightened stress levels on a day-to-day basis but at the same time are expected to function even more productively. He says that these stress hormones remain in the body for extended periods and actually need to be depleted for people to remain functional and adaptable to change.[1] So, sometimes the difficulty in being adaptable can, quite simply, be a physical reaction.

Here are some key reasons why being adaptable is important *now*:

- Advances in technology mean that we have got to keep learning and evolving, otherwise we will be left behind, quite literally. It's easy to be closed to social media surges, constantly changing devices and the demands that technology makes of us. Some of this is simple fear. But adaptability means being open to all and any changes that come into our lives, even embracing them. Steep learning curves only get steeper if you don't even attempt the ascent!

Stop and think!

How many times have you heard people say that Twitter is for twits? Yet, it is a hugely valuable business marketing tool that helps you to be right on top of your industry and profession. At the time of writing this text, 500,000 people join Twitter every day, and that is only set to increase.

- Remote work teams and telecommuting are fast becoming everyday. We need to learn how to adapt to communicating and working effectively in these new environments. Companies need to embrace cultural diversity, and cultural intelligence requires all of us to be far more adaptable than we currently are. Surprisingly, even the large multinationals still struggle with global diversity and adapting to different cultures.

- Multiple generations in the workplace and at home mean that we need to embrace different attitudes, ways of working and living. We are becoming less insular and more community-focused. This is being forced on us more than anything else, but is also a good thing. Truth is, our lifestyles have made us quite insular and self-focused. That is all being challenged and changed.

- We need to embrace innovation. There are many opportunities out there for those able to embrace and grab them. These opportunities will go to those who are flexible and adaptable enough to navigate their way. Opportunities happen by taking action and by being open enough in the first place to spot them.

● Many people are struggling with major changes to their lifestyles and work because of the economy, being made redundant or not being able to find work upon graduation. Changes such as living with parents for far longer than we'd like to, or suddenly finding ourselves without work but with many more years ahead of us where we want, and need, to work.

There's probably no other time in recent history where adaptability has been more important than it is right now!

So what sort of things make a person adaptable? The following are important:

1 **Intellectual flexibility** – this means keeping an open mind, being able to integrate new information smoothly and easily and switch easily from detail to the big picture.

2 **Being receptive** – especially to change! Being able to respond to change with positivity and being willing to try out new ways of doing something or looking at something. And overriding any initial resistance that may well be a very natural first response.

3 **Creativity** – actively seeking out new things and not being afraid to experiment or improvise.

4 **Communication style** – which can be adjusted to suit different contexts or situations. This means being much more aware of your own communication style and preference and being aware of which communication styles to adopt in different situations, even if these differ from your own natural style.

And the good news, again, is that all of these can be learned. Both nature and nurture affect our ability to be adaptable. Remember, adaptability has been present within the human race for millions of years. We all have this innately. Anything that hinders adaptability has been learned (see 'Barriers to being adaptable', later in this chapter) and so we may well have to *unlearn* some of this to get back in touch with our inner flexibility and natural openness.

> ## Stop and think!
>
> It's important to build adaptability incrementally. You'll be surprised by just how resistant to change you are! Next time you take part in a class or group event, try sitting in a different seat. Next time you go out to dinner, try a different food. Say 'yes' rather than 'no'. Your initial reaction definitely will be to not want to!

How can being adaptable help us at work?

We are surrounded by ambiguity, and today's workplace is full of changes, uncertainty and complexity. This is all being driven by changing workflow, processes, different kinds of internal reporting structures as well as the market environment and impact of technology. So the rules of how to succeed in this environment are changing too.

Businesses and people who are unable to or do not want to adapt will go the way of the dinosaur and will quietly be replaced by those who know how to and want to adapt to 'new school' challenges. The marketplace craves people who are flexible and adaptable and customers grow more demanding and informed every day.

> ## Stop and think!
>
> Ironically, it is often large businesses that struggle most with being adaptable and responding fast because there are so many layers of the organisation. Freelancer? Portfolio career or small business? You are in a unique position to be adaptable each and every day. And you'll need to be.

If you are adaptable you will be perceived as being effective, optimistic, supportive and proactively seeking solutions. If you are not adaptable, you could easily be perceived as being overwhelmed, resistant, stuck and resentful. Even if you aren't! I know how I'd rather be perceived.

In his book *Adaptability: The Art of Winning in an Age of Uncertainty*, strategy and innovation expert Max Mckeown argues that adaptability is now a threshold requirement for business survival because, as the pace of change quickens, companies are finding it harder and harder to keep up. He says the most successful adaptors are curious and they know that stability is actually a dangerous illusion. Did you know that Twitter was a 'plan B' produced by a struggling software company during an ad hoc brainstorm in a playground?

So adaptability is a key skill for a whole organisation to develop. Anne Loehr, leadership coach to large corporates, with a successful chameleon career herself, says: 'Success requires adaptation from leaders, and successful businesses embed adaptability into the foundations of their culture.'

In today's environment, when surrounded by highly intelligent and specialist-knowledge workers, trading on our old knowledge and skills, relying too much on our titles as a definition of our work and what we do and believing in job security are just not going to work any more. We need to adapt by continually evolving and reinventing ourselves. It means continuing to grow and transform and, in a way, become better versions of ourselves. This applies to every level in an organisation, and to each of us, regardless of what our job is; change or perish!

We also have to take on far more responsibility for this. We have to work harder now to create our own career paths and new opportunities. If the job for life is long gone, then being able to adapt and define our own job roles will be even more important. Employers today count adaptability as a key skill and it is often ranked as the highest, along with communication skills, interpersonal skills and a strong work ethic. In any job, in any company, you have to adapt to that company's culture and be able to 'fit in'.

People who are adaptable tend to be both flexible and versatile. And research shows that most people view themselves as being more flexible and adaptable than they really are. That's because we aspire to being flexible, open and adaptable. They are attractive traits. The Emotional Competence Inventory is a scientifically reliable test often used by employers during assessment panels.[2] It looks at different aspects of emotional intelligence and measures adaptability on four scales: openness to new ideas, adaptation to situations, handling of unexpected demands and adapting or changing strategy. Employers using this can start to gauge how adaptable an individual really might be, as opposed to their self-perception.

> you are very likely to perceive yourself as more adaptable and flexible than you really are

Working across different cultures in the workplace also makes demands of our adaptability skills. We need to be willing to accept and work with cultural differences and, the more adaptable we are, the easier that will be to do. But think about mental scripts (see later in this chapter) and we come smack up against possible prejudice and assumptions and not being as open as we might think to other cultures. Again, we all like to think that we are, but it's not necessarily the case deeper down.

Barriers to being adaptable

Even though we are hard-wired to be adaptable, we are also naturally resistant to change and this can stand in the way of being open to new experiences and opportunities. We also naturally fear rejection, so may shy away from doing something new or going out of our comfort zone for fear of being rejected.

Our mental scripts

Another barrier to being adaptable is to do with the way our brain processes any new information. It creates what is known as 'behavioural scripts' which basically are mental models that automate our actions.[3] An example is building a behavioural script for riding a bike. Through practice, this behaviour becomes entrenched and automatic until we can do it without thinking. Our brains will have lots of these scripts, from driving a car, speaking our mother tongue to even cooking a favourite dish. These scripts extend to other experiences and ways of doing things that we have learned. The scripts help us to be more efficient. They influence not only our actions but also what we see and believe.

> Adaptability is linked to youth and vitality. As we get older we develop more mental scripts, which can really challenge our ability to adapt to anything new. So by developing your adaptability skills you are tapping into agility, youth and new energy!

This efficiency also carries a downside, however, because the mental scripts can cause us to ignore the reality of a situation and dismiss any signals or new information because our brains already 'know what to do'. Mental scripts may also result in clinging stubbornly to the notion that 'this is how we have always done it', refusing to understand and accept the realities of a new situation. Henry Plotkin, a psychologist at University College in London, states that we tend to 'generalise into the future what worked in the past'. So, whatever worked in the past, we tend to do it or keep doing it; whatever didn't work, we tend to avoid.

Our mental scripts can make us rigid and unresponsive to change, as can work or other stress, which I've mentioned previously. Other barriers include being in competition with others and experiencing discontent or discomfort with a situation – usually this can also be traced back to fear or our mental scripts. What's important is to start to understand how they can impact our behaviour and cause us to be inflexible and not adaptable at all, however much we like to think that we are!

Lack of opportunity

There are always opportunities for us to test our adaptability skills but some of us may not actively seek these opportunities, and this in itself can be a barrier. If we have few opportunities growing up, to travel or try new things, then we may be even more resistant to this later in life. One of the reasons I want to start taking my five-year-old with me on some of my business trips to far-flung places, and the reason I've strongly encouraged my daughter to travel widely, is because many of these trips have, quite literally, opened my eyes. I have gone to places I would never have visited on holiday, or otherwise. I suppose one could also argue that maybe I would not have travelled to so many places others perceive as being unusual or high-risk, had I not been exposed to much travel and moving when I was younger. One of the reasons I am so adaptable is because I know I **can** adapt, having experienced different schools, different countries and having had to plunge in and learn a new language and make new friends. It's created a kind of fearlessness, which I feel very fortunate to have.

As a society in the West, though, we've become far more protective of our children. They are ferried everywhere by car, do not play in the streets and any travel is likely to be to holiday resorts far removed from the country's real culture. In the UK, most of our children do not even learn a foreign language! And I can remember well other parents' horror that I actively encouraged my daughter to navigate her way alone around the London Underground system at the age of 12. It meant that when she was a teenager, she was the one others relied on for getting around independently.

Is this over-protectiveness making our kids less adaptable and less equipped for what the world and life will throw their way? Does it make them less willing to seek out opportunities to stretch their comfort zones?

Stop and think!

Recently I travelled to Krakow in Poland, taking my husband and young son with me. Exploring the beautiful salt mines I remarked that just doing something completely out of the day-to-day routine is incredibly good for you and builds your skills of adaptability. So, whether it's travel or just taking a different route to work, if you're doing this kind of thing consistently you will become more adaptable.

Rigidity and fear

Fear is probably the biggest barrier to being adaptable. Fear of rejection, of failure, of circumstances, fear of change. This fear causes stress which creates physical responses that can actually prevent us from being flexible and open. It's as if those parts of ourselves simply shut down. This is why the expansion of our comfort zone is *so* crucial, because the more we experience that we can, and do, adapt, the more flexible and open we will be.

Can adaptability be developed?

'Individuals who cultivate a variety of skills seem brighter, more energetic and more adaptable than those who know how to do one thing only.'

Robert Shea

By learning how to be more adaptable, we also become better equipped to respond when faced with a life crisis. Resilient people often use these events as an opportunity to branch out in new directions.[4] While some people may be crushed by abrupt changes, highly resilient individuals are able to adapt and thrive. So how do we begin to develop this quality in ourselves and how can educators and trainers develop this in others? How can we make sure this is part of communication skills training, leadership training, or any kind of soft skills training?

Plastic brains

Neuroscience suggests that some people may be more adaptable than others. The brain is plastic and flexible, and now new brain circuits can be developed through parenting, education and training that nurture adaptability. Such interventions are thought to be more effective at crucial stages of our development, e.g. adolescence. So at the very stage in life where some of us may be very self-conscious about moving beyond our comfort zone, being encouraged to do so can have a permanent impact on how our brain develops, making us adaptable for life! Interestingly, I suppose life events can also make us more adaptable. For example, I left home completely at the age of 16 and moved house and school several times before that. My family life was disrupted on a regular basis through circumstances and factors completely beyond my control as a child and adolescent. Although these events were stressful in their way and not things that I even wanted, the experience of them at a time when my brain was still developing has made me lifelong adaptable, which I have always valued. Many of our young people in the West, growing up in relatively conventional households, need, therefore, to be given far more opportunities to stretch their comfort zones, whether that is through adventurous travel, volunteering work, trying out new sports and interests or by training and courses that increase their self-awareness of their own communication styles, ability to work in a team and their presenting and performance skills.

Opportunities for being adaptable are all around you

It can be as simple as looking for opportunities to try out new things and being open to new ideas. In small ways, such as going to the gym, we can exercise our adaptability muscles by changing plans at short notice, dealing with unexpected demands gracefully and calmly and doing something new, like singing or learning a new language. Both singing and learning a new language have other big fringe benefits. For singing: physical awareness, breathing control, presentation skills, listening skills, working as a team, performance skills and self-expression. For learning a foreign language: improving memory, protection against dementia, improving brain resilience, cultural awareness, differentiator at work and helping to understand communication styles.[5]

> every day there are opportunities for you to develop your adaptability skills

Experiential learning

Trainers and educators need to give people maximum opportunities to go out of their comfort zone through experiential learning, through 'real-play exercises' to encourage creativity and problem solving.[6] I think adaptability also needs to be better integrated into our education methods as an explicit skill. Many training exercises probably create stronger adaptability as an outcome, though this may not be explicit. We can also think about using comedy improvisation as a tool. I have a very talented American friend and associate, Jon Wilkerson, who uses the principles of improvisational theatre to help people move beyond their own mental scripts and barriers. I want to share with you some of the principles he teaches because they are so valuable to changing behaviour.

Improvisational theatre is a form of theatre popular in the United States. Instead of actors going on stage and performing memorised lines from a script, they must create a scene on the spot complete with fully developed characters, scintillating dialogue and a compelling environment. Life also has no script, which is why embracing these principles is so important.

To do this well, improvisational actors must be able to make bold choices, but they must also be quick to understand, accept, and support the choices of others. They must be able take on different roles with speed and commitment. They must be able to lead and to follow. They must have tremendous access to their creativity, but also must exercise judgement. They must be able to listen empathetically, but also to make quick reasoned decisions without second guessing themselves. They must be aware of their strengths and weaknesses and recover quickly from mistakes – even seeing them as opportunities. **These are the very same principles that allow a person to most effectively manage their own behaviour and accomplish their life goals.** These are also the skills of being truly adaptable.

Here are the principles; courtesy of Jon Wilkerson:[7]

- **Commitment** – means doing something with as much energy and enthusiasm as possible. When a comedy improvisational actor fails to commit on stage, the scene falls flat. When we fail to commit in life, our dreams grow dim. Whether we are applying for a job, leading a team on an important project, walking up to an important lead at a networking meeting, or asking someone on a romantic date, we need to take the plunge, to gather ourselves and jump with both feet into the situation with the firm intention to be the best that we can be. Improvisational actors *practise* commitment. That's why they are good at it.

- **Listening** – the ability to shut off the voices in our head and really pay attention to the people and environment around us. This can be very difficult to do when we are nervous and thinking about what we should do and say. However, by really giving attention to what our client, team member, or boss is saying, we can respond more appropriately than if we are constantly planning out our next sentence in our minds, or worrying whether we have a coffee stain on our sleeves!

- **Grabbing opportunities** – opportunities are fleeting and, if we don't jump on them fast, they will leave us behind, kicking ourselves. You know that feeling! I know it too. In improvisation, this is called 'accepting offers' and an 'offer' is defined as anything another actor says or does. That means *everything* is an opportunity! And if you are trained to do this you will see opportunities that others won't even notice.

- **Support** – a general attitude of helpfulness that all successful improvisational actors carry with them every moment they are on stage. It is also a common characteristic of anyone who is especially effective at his or her job, whether as a waiter or a CEO. These extraordinarily successful people know that support isn't just praising co-workers or being able to do what someone else is already doing. People who are adept at support know that real help is looking around and noticing what's *not* being done, and doing it! It means filling in what's missing. So to do this well, you need to be adept at listening, at grabbing opportunities and at committing.

- **Spontaneity** – the ability to act without over-thinking everything you do. It is having access to a sort of instantaneous judgement and being able to follow up on it immediately. It means not second-guessing all of your decisions. It requires good judgement that is built from experience, and it requires trust in your ability to recover quickly from bad decisions and learn from your errors. It is an essential companion to the other principles.

- **Fun** – what is fun? Fun is just fun! It means having a *positive attitude*, and leaning towards what you are doing and not away from it, or resisting it. When we head towards a challenge not only with a determination to succeed but with an expectation that tackling the challenge will be rewarding and fun, we run towards that challenge instead of stumbling towards it reluctantly.

10 steps to adaptability

The following steps can help you improve your adaptability skills and raise your general awareness, which is where everything must begin. Remember, it really is like exercising a muscle, and requires work!

1 **Open your mind**
   An open mind allows fresh ideas to come in and can help you with your plans and goals, because answers, ideas and solutions simply come more quickly to an open mind. It can help you see opportunities others might miss, discount or neglect. How to have an open mind? Challenge any limiting beliefs, become more aware of your own 'mental scripts' and challenge your own 'rut' thinking – if your way of responding to something is comforting, inviting and familiar, try changing it and see what happens!

2 **Stick at things**
   Being adaptable doesn't mean flitting from one thing to the next. Adaptability is closely linked to resilience, as well as perseverance. And resilient people stick at things. They keep going, even when the going gets tough. This is about your ability to concentrate, discipline and motivate yourself to complete a task or project. Strong application is underpinned by a sense of self-direction or free will, and these in themselves create robustness. As a consequence you are able to be more adaptable because you cope better with set-backs and rejection.

3 **Travel more**
   If you can afford to do so, take yourself and your family on an adventure! Even if you can't travel abroad, consider visiting different parts of your city or country where you perhaps would not normally consider going. Or go camping and try cooking and sleeping outdoors. Travel really does broaden your horizons.

4 **Be willing to learn**
We never really stop learning. Be willing to learn new methods, procedures and ways of doing things. Take on new tasks. Try something different. Draw conclusions from new information. And how about that foreign language you've always wanted to learn or that choir you've always wanted to join? It's easy to tell yourself you don't have time. But this is your life and it's not a dress rehearsal. Respond with energy to new challenges, the unfamiliar and the unexpected.

5 **Take yourself out of your comfort zone**
Look for opportunities to try new things that will keep you learning! You can do this in very small ways to start with – try learning a new skill, make new friends, try a new type of food, take the initiative for starting something in your community. As your comfort zone expands, make it bigger by doing more. Take on new challenges for work and seek them out. Embrace change, even if it feels uncomfortable at first. Reinvent yourself.

6 **Improvise**
Don't over-think and second-guess everything that you do. Practise being spontaneous – accept that last-minute invitation, change your weekend plans, walk into the presentation smiling with confidence knowing that you will do well (as long as you've put the preparation in, of course!). Grab that opportunity, it might not come again.

7 **Flex those muscles**
It's true that going to the gym will help you be more physically and mentally resilient, and we know that adaptability and resilience are linked, but I am talking about three types of flexibility: a) 'cognitive flexibility', using different thinking strategies and mental frameworks; b) 'emotional flexibility', varying your approach to dealing with your own emotions and those of others; and c) 'dispositional flexibility', remaining optimistic and at the same time realistic.[8] Look for as many opportunities as you

can to exercise these types of flexibility. The opportunities are all around you in your day-to-day life.

8 Adopt a 'can do' positive attitude to change

Even though it is natural to want to resist change, try and build up your ability to adapt and respond positively by literally changing your behaviour next time you are faced with a change. Again, start with small steps. You feel disappointed because of a change of plan? Respond enthusiastically even if you don't feel like doing so. Couldn't get tickets for a show you've been wanting to see? Smile and choose something completely different so you can embrace a new experience. Lost your job? Get upset, yes, but bounce back faster by taking positive action each and every day.

9 Get creative at problem solving

Research suggests that people who are able to come up with solutions to a problem are better able to cope with problems than those who can't. So, whenever you encounter a new challenge, make a quick list of some of the potential ways you could solve the problem. Experiment with different strategies and focus on developing a logical way to work through common problems. By practising these skills on a regular basis, you will be better prepared to cope when a serious challenge emerges.

10 Have a survivor attitude

Anything can be turned into a crisis or problem, if we want it to. Really, anything! Refuse to see yourself as a victim in any situation and always look for ways to resolve it. If you've always been quite a reactive person, this may be hard to do at first. Remember that you can never be in control of your circumstances and external events, you can only be in control of your own responses and behaviours. The trick is that if you focus on that, as opposed to the circumstances, chances are you'll influence the situation favourably anyway!

A day in the life of...

Let's take a magnifying glass to the skill of being adaptable through a day in the life of Fiona. We'll start with a brief introduction to Fiona, to give a quick snapshot of her life.

About Fiona

Fiona is a retired nurse and a widow. She has a small pension but is very concerned and worried about the future and how she will manage. Fiona lives in a small flat that she owns. She does a little part-time tutoring to supplement her pension but probably needs more money. She isn't able to afford holidays or travel, which she used to love. Her family all live overseas, including a daughter in Australia. She's lonely but doesn't like to admit this or show it. Fiona has a small network of friends she sees regularly and visits a local club where she exercises. She also uses the Internet, mainly for Skype and keeping in touch with her family.

Fiona is generally positive about things, even though she worries. She doesn't feel there is much she can do about her situation. She doesn't like thinking about her finances and so avoids this. She's in her early sixties and has only ever been a nurse. She believes she is 'too old' to learn anything new and will confirm this to herself through anything she reads or watches on TV. She feels very sad that she can't travel more and see more of her family. Most of the time she actually feels fairly bored. A long time ago she used to enjoy singing but never took it any further and doesn't read music. Her husband died around five years ago and Fiona misses him and seems to have got herself into a bit of a rut.

Let's have a closer look at a typical day in Fiona's life and how building the skill of being adaptable can help her.

Fiona's typical day

Fiona tends to get up very early and goes for a swim at her club before returning home for breakfast. She listens to a radio programme and does a bit of Sudoku and household chores before meeting a friend for lunch. This friend is busy starting a new flower-arranging business. Fiona is interested and compliments her friend on her talents. Fiona thinks to herself that she is 'not the sort of person to start a business' and that, anyway, even if she did have an idea for a new business, she doesn't have any money to get it going. Fiona tutors a nursing student at her flat mid-afternoon, which she quite enjoys as it keeps her active in the nursing profession. After that she does some gardening and then cooks dinner and watches a little TV.

Today Fiona also runs into a couple of other friends. She bumps into one who has just started singing with a local community choir where no auditions or sight-reading is required. Her friend encourages Fiona to join but Fiona feels very timid about the whole idea of singing again and decides not to. Then she stops to chat with another friend. They chat about how terrible the weather has been and how soon the nights will be drawing in and there hasn't been much of a summer.

Fiona often surfs the Net of an evening or Skypes her family. She was supposed to be meeting up to go to the cinema with an old work colleague this evening but at the last minute was let down. The outing was planned some time ago and so Fiona felt very disappointed by this and spent the evening at home alone.

What's going on here?

Fiona's life is ticking along but she doesn't sound terribly happy. On the surface her life seems to be active but actually it's almost as if life is passing her by. She doesn't seem to be making the most of her potential. She has adapted to her life as a widow, yes, but she is not in herself adaptable enough to make more of her life. Yet she is only in her early sixties and there are many many good years ahead of her. She appears to have given up and be resigned to her life as it is now. At the same time she is slightly envious of her friends who seem to be involved in new things and leading busy lives and have somehow reinvented themselves. Fiona probably also feels a little isolated as her family lives overseas and she is unable to afford the travel to see them. She is worried about money and about her future, yet doesn't see herself in a position to do anything about it as her 'working life' has stopped. Her life could be so much happier if she exercised the skill of adaptability. She might be able to earn some extra cash and even save for a trip. Fiona is also quite bored – she has an active mind but isn't really exploiting that and she seems to be living the life of someone much older than she actually is. She likes to plan ahead but she has lost touch with being spontaneous.

If Fiona puts some of the ideas about adaptability into practice, it could all look quite different.

Let's revisit Fiona's 'typical day' six months later.

How Fiona's life has moved forward

Fiona was able to visit her daughter in Australia, as her family kindly paid for this visit. The trip came as a welcome surprise and, although it wasn't planned ahead as Fiona would have preferred, the desire to see her family was strong enough to override this initial discomfort. While she was in Australia, Fiona had sufficient distance from her life to really think about some of the things she wanted to change. The trip away was refreshing and energising for her. She decided to spend a little time taking stock and putting together a plan for herself. Her part-time tutoring is rewarding and Fiona decided to try and do more of this. She offered her services at the local nursing training college, starting with taster sessions. This soon led to a regular group of student nurses wanting group tutoring, which is more cost-effective for them and means Fiona now has regular additional income.

Fiona's day is now spent more actively. In the mornings she is busy putting together revision materials for nursing students, which she plans to compile and offer through a new website she wants to develop. It's early days but she is hopeful that this may be another source of income. She continues to meet her friends but spends more time with friends who are active in various things and this gives her great support with what she is working on. Fiona has also taken more control over her finances by getting some sound financial advice. She has started to save a little money on a regular basis and is planning to take a short weekend trip soon with one of her friends. She also often meets friends at short notice – after all she is not on a fixed schedule and has no family ties.

Fiona generally feels more relaxed and happy about life, which means that now she really enjoys her time gardening, cooking or surfing the Net. Whereas, before, these activities felt a little functional, she now feels there is more purpose to them. She has started to try out new recipes and grow new types of vegetables. She finds that the more she focuses on the things she is able to do, the more productive and relaxed she feels, and the wider her comfort zone becomes. It's tremendously energising. She feels less lonely and has things to look forward to. She's even thinking about taking a course for starting up small businesses, as well as learning more about using the Internet.

She decided to give the choir a try too. She felt nervous initially, but found it helpful to think about all the new things she had been doing lately and then this no longer felt so daunting.

Adaptability is a skill we can all benefit from. It's not only something that can help you adjust to major life changes and upheaval, but it can also make your life happier and more interesting in the day to day. By becoming more adaptable day to day you will be better equipped to deal with bigger changes that come your way. Because they will! And you may want them to.

Interested in reading more?

Buch, K. (2009) 'Adaptability – Leading Through Focused Conversations'. You can download this article from www.managementconcepts.com, www.astd.org or from www.the-advantage.info

Mckeown, M. (2012) *Adaptability: The Art of Winning In An Age of Uncertainty*. Kogan Page

Ryan, M.J. (2009) *AdaptAbility: How To Survive Change You Didn't Ask For*. Broadway Books

You can also find more tips, ideas and exercises by visiting www.the-advantage.info

'Not everything that counts can be counted and not everything that can be counted counts.'

William Bruce Cameron

Chapter 2

CRITICAL THINKING

W e're familiar with critical thinking from our university days. It's what you are meant to be doing, after all, alongside all the partying. But now, the current harsh economic conditions and competitive environment demand from all of us a rethink of critical thinking, as well as the ability to effectively develop and hone these skills in ourselves.

What is critical thinking?

At a simple level, critical thinking means making an evaluation or judgement about what we see or hear about facts or a situation presented to us. For many people, this means making a quick mental decision in a fairly short space of time. Although this works most of the time, critical thinking is much more than this. It's about questioning assumptions, evaluating a situation from different angles, solving problems creatively and using a reflective, considered approach. We have become used to using a 'light' approach, though. We all lead incredibly busy lives and information comes to us in lots of different ways. The way we look at information on websites and social media has also contributed to this 'speed' in making judgements and how we perceive data. Attention is a hot commodity in our world. And attention is also a vital component of being able to think critically in a way that benefits us.

There is sufficient evidence to suggest that our graduates do not come out of university with strong critical thinking skills and, even more, that the current type of learning and teaching at university does not really encourage critical thinking in depth.[1] For example, students who study courses entitled 'Critical Thinking' are more likely to learn how to label certain types of thinking than how to actually think critically for themselves and relate this to their own work, life and goals.

On a deeper level, our ability to think critically and solve problems creatively is being challenged by our changing world environment. Unfortunately, a thinking skills explosion has not accompanied the information explosion.[2] Yet, if you want to succeed in twenty-first-century business, the ability to think critically is vital because as the huge growth and abundance of information increases on a daily basis, managing this amount of information has become much more difficult. We have a real problem of information overload, which has led to shorter attention spans and an inability to manage this information effectively.

Stop and think!

Did you know, for example, that at the time of writing this text we see an average of 34 billion bits of information online, or the equivalent of 2 books' worth per day.[3] Since this information explosion is only set to increase, hadn't we better get back in touch with those critical thinking skills?

Why is critical thinking so important?

According to the American Management Association's 2010 'Critical Skills Survey', there are four 'C' skills essential for a company's success:

1 **Critical thinking and problem solving** – the ability to make decisions, solve problems and take appropriate action.

2 **Communication** – the ability to synthesise and transmit ideas, both verbally and in writing.

3 **Collaboration and team building** – working effectively with others, including people with different points of view and with diverse groups.

4 **Creativity and innovation** – being able to see what is missing and fix it.

The most important skill defined was critical thinking, and all of these skills were felt to be absolutely crucial in the next few years.

The US Department of Labor identified the skill of critical thinking as 'raw material' for a number of key workplace skills, such as problem solving, decision making, organisational planning and risk management. These are the skills deemed to be essential for avoiding mistakes and miscalculations. Lack of critical thinking can lead to evaluating market and needs inaccurately through preconceived notions and assumptions. Quite often, too, people at the top of an organisation are automatically assumed to be bright and 'good' thinkers, so the ability to think critically tends not to be assessed or measured the higher up an organisation you go. Critical thinking is even more important when sophisticated decision making and judgement are needed.

> lack of critical thinking skills can lead to dangerous miscalculations, unproven assumptions and poor decision making

Dr Linda Elder, an educational psychologist and an authority on critical thinking, defines the process as 'self-guided, self-disciplined thinking which attempts to reason at the highest level of quality in a fair-minded way. People who think critically consistently attempt to live rationally, reasonably, empathically.'[4]

Using this definition and applying it, for example, to marketing, it's possible to make better decisions related to a company's public perception. If you package a product appealing to certain demographic groups based on stereotypical assumptions, then that really isn't a great marketing tactic. But it happens all the time, nevertheless. Recently, at a farmer's market in my hometown, I wanted to buy some regional beer. The business owner told me that if I chose right I 'might get more housekeeping money'. Several assumptions were being made here all at once: I was buying the beer for my husband. I was married. I didn't drink beer. I didn't work. And so on. I didn't make a purchase. To apply Elder's definition to marketing, it's important to create more widespread appeal, regardless of the target market's likely gender, ethnicity and other characteristics. So marketing must use critical thinking skills to think beyond a 'target profile'.

The same can be said of customer service and sorting out problems. Product knowledge and understanding of the customer's needs and problems are a part of that, as well as having the autonomy to solve a problem and use a self-guided process to arrive at a solution.

Critical thinking has also been proven to have a positive impact on creativity. A study by Nusbaum and Silvia in 2011 found that people high in fluid reasoning (closely connected to critical thinking) outperformed others in creative ideas.[5] Why is creativity important? Because creativity contributes to having fresh new ideas and being able to take the initiative amidst uncertainty. Creativity gives organisations and individuals the competitive advantage – it's the one thing that makes each of us unique. And critical thinking plays a key part.

critical thinking and creativity are a match made in heaven!

The majority of cognitive ability tests include critical thinking. Such tests are used more now by companies, so you may be asked to take one at your next job interview. Increasingly these tests are now being seen as the strongest and most consistent predictors of job performance, leadership effectiveness and creativity. The main reason these tests are so powerful is because they predict both what you can do right now and the extent to which you are likely to learn and develop in the future (Kuncel & Hezlett).

Ellen Kumata, a consultant to Fortune 200 companies has this to say: 'The idea that a company's senior leaders have all the answers and can solve problems by themselves has gone completely by the way-side... The person who's close to the work has to have strong analytical skills. You have to be rigorous: test your assumptions, don't take things at face value, don't go in with preconceived ideas that you're trying to prove.' This means that the need for far stronger critical thinking skills is relevant for every employee at every level of an organisation.

Employers want employees who can think independently and autonomously, problem solve, use good judgement and make decisions. Decisions are often made at work without reflection or without all the key facts required to make a wise choice or judgement, because a decision is needed quickly. And if you think about it, you are probably expected to make decisions a lot faster these days. That's OK isn't it? We make quick decisions all the time. Well, yes it probably is fine for much of the time, especially if you are able to apply a wider or deeper set of experiences to inform your decision, but it simply isn't a good idea where outcomes are critical. A good example of where critical thinking is very important is in project management. Without sufficient attention to detail, working out costs, resources, time management, team roles and priorities, a project in most industries will fail.

David Garvin of the Harvard Business School told *The New York Times*, 'I think there's a general feeling that people need to sharpen their thinking skills, whether it's questioning assumptions, or looking at problems from multiple points of view.'[6]

And it's especially important now, with companies facing huge challenges with global competition (including small businesses), emerging markets, technology changes and the political and economic landscape. Employees at every level, entrepreneurs, leaders and managers need to be able to think fast and act smart – often in situations that are complex, uncertain and where there might not already be an effective policy or existing procedure in place. All this means critical thinking is vital, and it also means that these critical thinking skills have an added layer of challenge to them.

Stop and think!

As the rate of complexity rises, the need for critical thinking is resurfacing. Richard Paul of the Center for Critical Thinking says: 'Critical thinking, if somehow it became generalised in the world, would produce a new and very different world, a world which increasingly is not only in our interest but is necessary to our survival.'

OK, so why does it matter to you?

In the current climate, you may well be one of the many people who are simply overwhelmed by work overload, information overload and stress. Yet strong critical thinking and problem-solving skills are the very ones that are going to be able to help you manage these problems and work and live smarter; skills such as rationality, self-awareness, honesty, open-mindedness, discipline and judgement, and the ability to be an active thinker, a sceptical thinker, to question, to analyse, in depth and faster than ever before.

We need to be able to question assumptions far more and seek out the *what* and the *why* of every situation. We need to be able to adopt different perspectives and have a much greater awareness of cultural differences. These are deductive skills. But good critical thinkers also need to be creative and be able to see opportunities where others might only see obstacles. So they need to be looking for solutions rather than for problems and this is much more than mere 'problem solving'.

In a world of growing uncertainty one thing is certain: we will need sharp critical thinkers who can size up the situation, realise the potential where others may not or cannot, and seize opportunities through prompt decision making. The good news is that our brains definitely have the capacity to develop effective critical thinking skills. It is a purely cognitive skill and there are exciting developments that inform how we can improve our critical thinking skills. There are three, in particular, that are important to note:

1 **Inhibitory control** – the ability to resist the strong inclination to do one thing in order to do something else that is more appropriate, or would better help you to reach a goal. This is important because it means that even if we feel like sleeping because we are tired, or putting off an important project, we are able to resist this and choose behaviour that helps us get something done. This is well-documented research that proves we are able to control or regulate our behaviour, so there's no excuse! (Diamond *et al* 2007.)

2 **Working memory** – a mental 'jotting pad' feature of your brain that shares important information that you can use in the course of everyday life, helping you stay focused on a task, block out distractions and keep you aware (Gathercole and Packiam-Alloway 2008).

What this means is that it is now proven that there is a feature in our brain that is critical to our ability to control our attention, concentrate despite distractions, successfully multitask, learn and comprehend what we read and generally improve our overall performance on measures of intelligence.

Historically, it was believed that working memory was actually a fixed ability that could not be improved and, even worse, that it declined with age. This new research proves this all wrong. And that is good news!

There are lots of methods and techniques for improving your working memory, which we will come back to at the end of this section.

3 **Cognitive flexibility** – 'ability to stay on track is an asset, but being dead on the track is not' (Goldberg 2001). Cognitive flexibility is our human ability to switch behavioural responses according to the context of a situation. The ability of a person to see different aspects of an idea or situation and switch their 'attentional set' can now be measured through neuropsychological tests and improved through training.

> it's more than a collection of techniques – it is a mind-set, lifestyle and more focused way of thinking

Being a critical thinker is a lot more than learning a collection of techniques, though. It is a mind-set, an attitude and a way of thinking that you adopt and apply on a consistent basis, every day. Becoming a better critical thinker is a bit like becoming a better athlete. We are all born with the ability to move, but to develop our athletic skills we need to learn technique and practise. People who are athletic are usually good at multiple sports but excel at one or two. Critical thinkers also approach most problems effectively but excel in specific areas. The decision to build your athletic skills is a lifestyle decision. To be a competent athlete you need to live a healthy and active lifestyle. Likewise, critical thinking is also a lifestyle issue. Critical thinkers approach every situation by trying to evaluate it accurately and make the best possible decision at the time.

> becoming a better critical thinker is a bit like becoming a better athlete

How is critical thinking changing?

Critical thinking has a long academic tradition and history, having its roots in philosophy and using deep reflection to help to understand our existence. The fundamentals of critical thinking in terms of gathering good evidence, separating facts from opinions and questioning and drawing sound conclusions by applying logical deduction are all well known. These skills can be analysed and discussed from a number of different perspectives and, indeed, this has been done widely and there are numerous studies and research articles to support this. Most of the traditional material on critical thinking is presented either from an academic angle or a psychological one (cognitive focus). More recently, neuroscience has contributed to a better understanding of critical thinking in terms of how our brains work and the patterns involved.

The University of Phoenix's non-profit Institute for the Future has published some extensive research entitled 'Work Skills 2020' which underpins key drivers that are currently shaping our future.

It is worthwhile looking at six current principles to underpin why we need to rethink our critical thinking skills and how some of the features of critical thinking are changing.

1. How we make sense of things

This is the ability to determine the deeper meaning or significance of what is being expressed. In our fast-moving world this requires a reflective, considered approach that does not come easily. For example, today, anyone can publish anything on the Internet and much of this information is actually flawed, biased or possibly even inaccurate. We need sharper critical thinking skills to discern the information we are constantly bombarded with and to remember that 'Googling' something is not the same as researching and understanding it properly.

Stop and think!

How often do you question the first result that comes up when you Google something? You probably take it at face value because it came up in the first page of results. But that doesn't mean it's valuable, well written or even accurate!

The way we work is changing: as manufacturing and service jobs are automated there is an increasing demand for the kinds of skills that machines are not good at – yet. These are higher-level thinking skills (critical reasoning skills – numerical, verbal and spatial) that as yet cannot be codified. So we need to be ready in ways we haven't been in the past. Just think for one minute about all the massive technological changes just in the last ten years. This isn't stopping any time soon and is, in fact, accelerating!

As it becomes a reality that machines might take over from human labour, critical thinking or sense making are the skills workers will need to capitalise on.

2. Novel and adaptive thinking is needed more than ever

Earlier we explored all the trends and changes that are impacting us. Critical thinking now includes adaptive thinking because most jobs demand what is known as 'situational adaptability' – the ability to respond to unique, unexpected circumstances of the moment. In addition, given high rates of rising unemployment, everyone will need to up their ability to respond effectively. We are now experiencing job polarisation: middle-skill white-collar and blue-collar jobs are declining due to automation of routine work and global offshoring. On the other hand, job opportunities are increasingly concentrated in both high-skill, high-wage technical and management occupations and in low-skill, low-wage occupations, such as foods service and personal care. Jobs at the high end involve abstract tasks and, at the low-skill end, manual tasks. This trend will accelerate increasing societal inequalities.

3. Computational thinking is on the increase

This is the ability to translate vast amounts of data into abstract concepts and to understand data-based reasoning. Many more roles will require computational thinking skills in order to make sense of the vast amounts of information. This is already happening, and most people already feel huge amounts of pressure in their day-to-day work. It's only going to increase, so get used to it! Computational thinking will help. And it probably means learning to use more of our brains more effectively. It has been estimated that we actively use only about 10 per cent of our brains, which surely means we have the capacity to do far more. From neuroscience we know that there are individual learning differences with the basis in the brain. We also know that it's possible to improve critical reasoning skills.

4. New media literacy is required

This is the ability to critically assess and develop content that uses new media forms, and to leverage these media for persuasive communication. We have an explosion in user-generated media, including the videos, blogs and podcasts that now dominate our social lives, and this will be felt fully in workplaces over the next few years. Those who do not embrace these new media, or do not know how to use and manage them to the best effect, will simply be left behind.

5. Managing our cognitive load

This is the ability to discriminate and filter information for importance, and understand how to maximise cognitive functioning using a variety of tools and techniques. Given the way we work is changing and the sheer amounts of information we are expected to understand, coupled with the distraction of social media and the Internet, this ability is crucial. We also have to learn how to unlearn our bad habits of what we think is multi-tasking but, in reality, is lessening our ability to retain key information.

6. Becoming T-shaped

This is a literacy in and an ability to understand concepts across multiple disciplines. The ideal future worker is 'T-shaped' – they bring deep understanding of at least one field, but have the capacity to converse in the language of a wider depth and breadth of fields. Lifelong learning will be of paramount importance in parallel with extended life spans. Let's face it, we are all going to be working for a lot longer than we thought! So critical thinking and reasoning across different topics, subjects, specialist fields and disciplines will become more important, and those who rise to this challenge will have a competitive edge.

All of the above points to significant gaps in our current ways of learning and absorbing information, as well as our education

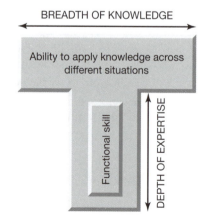

Shape of the ideal future worker

systems. If the world of work is changing like this, our education system needs to be better prepared to equip our young people to flourish in it. And those of us no longer in the education system need to be prepared and ready to expand our thinking and life-long learning skills.

Barriers to developing critical thinking

Perhaps the main barrier to developing effective critical thinking has been a lack of awareness of what it actually is and how important it is as a skill. In academic terms there is still a stigma to critical thinking training in that it is stuffy, too academic to be engaging and that it's an abstract concept. It certainly does not seem to be mainstream, just yet.

Creative problem solving sounds like more fun and is something that educators and trainers will happily include in sessions. Perhaps now, though, given the need for our critical thinking skills themselves to change, this brings yet more scope for a teacher or trainer to introduce a whole range of new types of exercises. To start with, we probably need to work on our own critical thinking skills each and every day.

So the barriers are more to do with the way we define critical thinking and the way it is currently taught academically.

On top of this we can be prone to making assumptions about any and every situation without necessarily having all the relevant information. We can easily make assumptions based on our own perception of a situation or issue without making sure we have all the background facts first. The media encourages this to a certain extent also with big headlines, leading photographs and possibly biased or insufficient information. So it can also be quite tricky to get right if we are expected to think critically with speed, and with even more information at our fingertips.

There are other barriers to be aware of that are things we naturally do, almost without realising it. It's useful to look at these in more detail.

Confirmation bias

This is when we take the evidence or information presented to us and deliberately look for components that support our point of view, instead of being objective. This is a completely natural tendency and quite hard to fight unless you do the exact opposite and actively try and seek out information that doesn't support your own beliefs.

Attribution bias

This is a basic belief that good things happen because of internal factors and bad things because of external factors. This can cause us to pigeonhole actions of others, especially when it comes to negative behaviour, to being the fault of the individual and not the circumstances. And we'll do this almost subconsciously.

Trusting hearsay

This is all about believing information someone else gives us, even if there is no evidence to support it. We tend to take things at face value, especially gossip. And how willing are we to select a product or service based on others' recommendations? Word of mouth is the strongest marketing tool, but it can also be a danger to our ability to think critically and independently if we take everything we hear from others at face value.

Memory lapses

No, this is nothing to do with having a 'senior moment' or any other type of memory lapse. This is more to do with the common human trait of 'filling in the gaps' with our own information or ideas, which may or may not be accurate. When we recall an experience or when we are explaining a problem, we'll often put our own spin on it and where any information is missing, or we don't remember it completely, we'll fill in the gaps quite naturally.

Accepting authority without question

In the sixties, famous experiments were conducted by the social psychologist Stanley Milgram where people were willing to administer ever more powerful shocks on the orders of an authority figure, even though they were not convinced it was right to do so.[7] And this failure to think critically can continue to be seen in blind acceptance of people with 'expertise', or in positions of power and authority.

Not admitting you don't know all the facts

None of us likes to look foolish in front of others. This trait can sometimes lead to quite wild fabrication and speculation! It's better to just admit you don't know something rather than 'fake' knowledge. It happens much more often than we think and can sometimes happen automatically through over-elaborating on facts, or by telling 'white lies' to appear more knowledgeable than we are.

Can critical thinking be developed?

Yes it can! The skills you need to get ahead are based on a combination of natural ability through character traits and genetics and cognitive flexibility, meaning they are connected with how our brain functions. By understanding our character traits and developing our self-awareness we can build these skills through changing our behaviour. By strengthening our brain and having a better understanding of how it works, we can also build the seven skills.

Critical thinking IS a pure cognitive function – deeply connected with our brain. It's really about a process: asking questions and then asking more, depending on the answers we get. It's about practising discipline and being more rigorous. Yet, as we can see from the barriers described, other character traits and human tendencies can interfere significantly with our ability to think critically.

Flex your thinking

If empathy is also part of developing critical thinking, as Linda Elder suggests in her book *30 Days to Better Thinking and Better Living with Critical Thinking*, then the more 'intuitive' process of considering another's point of view, including emotions, opinions, background, knowledge and intentions, is, to some extent, hard-wired for many people.

Maria Garcia Winner, a leading specialist in social-cognitive defects, believes that how we think is inextricably linked to how we feel.[8] Social thinking is, basically, what we do when we interact with other people. Critical thinking, although an individual skill, is rarely conducted in isolation. Winner outlines these key elements of social thinking:

1   Our thoughts and emotions are strongly connected. How we think affects how we feel and how we feel affects how we think. We may not want that to be the case, but it is. Therefore, we need to know how to manage our emotions and thoughts effectively.

2   We think about others, even if we have no intention of interacting with them. We adjust our behaviour based on what we think others may be thinking about us. This is not based on anything factual! Only our own perception.

3   We 'think with our eyes' in order to figure out other people's thoughts, intentions and emotions. We read other people's faces and interpret what they are thinking from their expressions. Most of the time we'll also, often wrongly, go even further and attribute our perception of what they may be thinking or feeling to something we have said and done.

Winner says that when people learn how to think differently and flexibly, they can think anywhere. And probably be happier as a result too.

By far the best way to build critical thinking skills is within how we educate young people. Building self-determination skills, such as goal setting, decision making, self-advocacy and problem solving, should all be included in career planning for young people. Critical thinking skills can also be taught from a very young age onwards.

Developing cognitive flexibility is seen as key to unlocking critical thinking in our brains. Cognitive flexibility is our human ability to switch how we behave according to the context of the situation. This is done by ensuring that the learning of any subject is within a flexible learning environment.[9] This means that the knowledge presented should be done so in a variety of different ways and for different purposes. The more information added to a task, the more our competences are challenged. They need to be challenged for us to tap into our critical thinking skills.[10]

Do you run or do you fight? Let's say you know you are physically fit and could box someone in a ring and win. But faced with an unknown opponent in the street, late at night, who is shorter than you, you may need to use some critical thinking. And supposing you have also had a drink? Doesn't make the process any easier does it? It's clear, though, that in one situation we may evaluate something a certain way but in another quite differently. And we need to become more nimble and agile in this process.

Clinical psychologists Lauren Kenworthy and Benjamin Yerys say that cognitive flexibility is best taught to young children through a hierarchy of other skills, including physical flexibility (such as Yoga and spatial games), coping skills and recognising feelings, introducing 'heroes' and creating clear goals. And forward-thinking primary schools often include such experiential learning. Unfortunately, this seldom continues once children reach adolescence.

Cognitive flexibility is so important to developing strong critical thinking skills because it gives us the ability to adjust nimbly to changing demands and priorities and it requires consistent consideration of new perspectives, new information and adjusting to change. If you're a flexible thinker you are far more likely to find lots of different ways to problem solve, accept other ideas and try out new things. You won't be thrown by rapid changes, unexpected curve balls or even annoying people.

Improve your mental jot pad – your working memory

This is critical to your ability to control your attention, concentrate despite distractions, successfully multi-task, learn and comprehend what you read and generally improve your overall performance on measures of intelligence. And it improves with age! There is now even software that can make you smarter. Dual-N Back training is software that gives you a mental workout by getting you to keep track of objects on a screen while, at the same time, keeping the sequence of auditory letter sounds.[11] As you train, you progressively improve your ability to hold more information in your working memory.

Chess also improves working memory because you tend to play out sequences in your mind first and you maintain them on your mental jotting pad as you analyse the various options. In one study of older people, chess was found to be the single activity most predictive in reducing the risk of mental decline. The same goes for reading books and, the more complex the material you are reading, the higher the load on your working memory.

Dopamine has been shown to improve working memory and this can be sourced easily in eating the right kinds of foods such as carbohydrates (pasta, rice, potatoes), avocados, bananas, pumpkin seeds, leafy green vegetables, fish and poultry.

you are what you eat, quite literally, it seems!

Take on the barriers to critical thinking

Next time you find yourself in a situation where you reflexively resort to filling in any gaps with your own assumptions, or automatically listen out for opinions and information that support your own viewpoint, or take what you hear at face value, stop a moment and take stock. The more you can spot your weaknesses the more self-aware you will become. Don't forget that these are completely natural tendencies that we all do and, mostly, are wired to do. The more we can rise above these tendencies and fight, the more strategies we will develop for thinking critically.

10 steps to critical thinking

The following steps can help you improve your critical thinking skills and raise your general awareness, which is where everything must begin. Remember, it really is like exercising a muscle and requires work! Using a journal to record your thoughts and experiences, even for a short amount of time, is very helpful.

1 **Question assumptions**

Wherever the assumptions come from, question them. Critical thinkers are curious and look to find the what and the why behind everything. Become more forensic when presented with a situation and try to work out where assumptions are being made. We probably make them so automatically in so many situations without thinking. Well, now is the time to change that and to ask why.

2 **Adopt different perspectives**
Get into other peoples' heads as much as you can! This is where empathy comes in. Involve others in decision making too. If you are fortunate enough to be working in a culturally diverse environment, find out how others might view a problem. You will uncover valuable insights.

3 **Use data to drive decisions**
Replace any guesswork or gaps with facts and data, and challenge decisions that have materialised without any data or facts to support them. Always do your homework and check everything. And if you're not sure of something, say so, and find out.

4 **Learn how to deal with ambiguity**
You may like things to be crystal clear, but the speed of life, business intertwined with global factors, technology and people included in the mix mean that you might never know all the variables. So you need to get comfortable with operating in an environment where change is constant and fast decisions are required.

5 **Get creative**
See opportunities where others see obstacles and seek these out! A savvy smart thinker views setbacks and issues as opportunities for something new, or as a way to do things better. Explore new ways of being creative and innovative. You don't have to be a 'creative person' – your brain naturally has the ability to think creatively.

6 **Build in reflection time**
It will always seem like there is not enough time for this, but make time for reflection anyway and make thinking and reflection a priority in any decision-making process. You can build in reflection time to your day – even five-minute

pockets here and there can make a difference because a little more time allows for this careful thought process and better decision making to occur and become more of a default setting.

7 Get past face value
Don't settle for surface impressions, or 'gut feeling'. Think about root factors and source issues and about what is really going on underneath. Don't believe everything you hear, not for a minute! We tend to do this so automatically, though. Oh, and whatever you do, don't gossip!

8 Build your skills
Read, read, read and, better still, write or blog. Have more in-depth conversations on important complex topics. Explore current events more. Get involved in debates. Have a view and an opinion. Learn something new every day. Keep learning, keep curious. If you have children, encourage them to do the same.

9 Stop pigeonholing
We make automatic judgements of others based on quite loose 'facts'. Train yourself to stop doing this, even if you only do it in jest. What comes out of your mouth gets remembered, not just by others but also by your brain. Pretty soon you'll actually believe your own judgements yourself, without testing their reliability.

10 Be honest and open
Communicate clearly, don't fabricate and don't fake knowledge. Prepare properly for meetings and presentations so you don't have to 'fill in the gaps' based on your poor preparation. Slow down a little and don't take on so much. Take the time to do things properly and well.

A day in the life of...

Let's take a magnifying glass to the skill of critical thinking through a day in the life of Lisa. We'll start with a brief introduction to Lisa, to give a quick snapshot of her life.

About Lisa

Lisa is in her twenties, a young entrepreneur with her own Internet fashion business, which is starting to become quite successful. She travels a lot for work and doesn't have a fixed office as such – everything is run from home and, as she is often on the move, she works mainly with her laptop, tablet device and smartphone. Lisa says she can work anywhere at any time and feels fortunate to have such a flexible business. Lisa spends a lot of her time interacting with virtual teams and with suppliers and buyers in the Middle East and Asia.

Lisa is energetic and extrovert and generally upbeat. She has a wide network of friends and she's very active on social media, both personally and through her business. She doesn't tend to read much and feels that she can get whatever she needs online. She started her business straight out of university. She'd always had a flair for fashion and her History degree, although interesting enough, did not really equip her for the world of work – so she's had to learn everything by doing it, and very fast. To her credit, she's built up a successful and thriving business.

Let's have a closer look at a typical day in Lisa's life and how building her critical thinking skills can help her.

Lisa's typical day

Lisa tends not to keep set hours. She gets up late and often works late into the night, because of time differences and also because being active on the fashion scene at evening shows and nightclub events requires this. Once up, she tends to get straight to her computer or iPad, checking email, Twitter, Facebook and other social media and flitting from the business to the personal and back again. Actually, she is constantly distracted by her Twitterfeed and articles and news she clicks onto. Once Lisa is up in the morning, it's often close to lunchtime so she tends to drink only coffee and then grab a salad for lunch. During lunch she hosts a conference call with suppliers and buyers. The afternoon is taken up with admin and setting up meetings. She books flights to Hong Kong and a hotel mid-afternoon. She then is presented with a bit of a crisis in that one of her suppliers can't meet a critical deadline. She immediately discusses this with her virtual team but they're unable to resolve this easily because of the overlap with other orders and deadlines. Lisa finds this very stressful and decides she will deal with this tomorrow, when she's had some time to think about it.

Lisa's social life tends to blend with her work. This evening, like most, she goes to a networking and media event that is combined with a business dinner. She gets into a conversation with one of her competitors, which doesn't go very well, and Lisa feels a bit discouraged but shrugs it off. Her business is doing great.

Lisa leaves the event and goes home in the early hours. Before bed she rechecks her email and Twitterfeed to make sure she hasn't missed anything before falling into a fitful sleep.

What's going on here?

Lisa is young and energetic and has, what sounds like, a thriving business. She's done really well to start it straight out of university and she obviously has entrepreneurial skills, which is great. At first glance it may not be easy to see how critical thinking skills might help her. Surely she got enough of that on her History degree? But what is happening, is that Lisa doesn't have the critical thinking skills that could make her and her business really flourish. She is in danger of burning out too because, as her business grows, so will the demands on her time and, at the moment, she doesn't have any structure to her day and is unable to manage the overload of information and data she is bombarded with day-to-day. Because of the constant online distractions, her brain is starting to become weaker at focusing and giving attention to any one task, making her really quite inefficient. Critical thinking would help her to work more effectively with social media. In her industry, too, innovation and creativity are high on the list of top competences that critical thinking can boost significantly. Critical thinking can also help Lisa problem solve more effectively and creatively, which doesn't always happen. And the reason why that conversation with her competitor didn't go well? Lisa is not the greatest listener because her attention flits. In this instance, because she wasn't really focusing on the other person, her brain leapt into gear and gave her lots of assumptions and 'missing information' to plug those gaps where she wasn't focused.

Lisa decides to put some of the ideas on critical thinking into practice. Let's revisit Lisa's 'typical day' six months later.

How Lisa's life has moved forward

These days Lisa has a much better grip on social media. She's decided to use it more to the advantage of the business by becoming an expert in her field – she's doing this by blogging on a regular basis, which requires her to research quality content. So she is starting to process some of the information and data coming at her online in a more orderly way. Writing the blog is enabling her to connect different ideas and see their relevance

– in fact it reminds her of some of the coursework she did on her History degree, which she enjoyed a lot. Lisa also keeps her professional and personal social media activity separate. Although this has not been easy for her to do, she has recognised its importance. She now keeps social media activity to set times of the day and has set up a social media dashboard to make it easier to manage the various feeds and posts. Because of the blog, though, her posts are becoming more strategic anyway. Gradually, she is starting to plan her activity and focus on specific areas at different times of the day – i.e. blog and industry research, posting about events, marketing activity, photography and image posts.

Lisa has decided to build in more creativity sessions with the teams she works with. She has realised how crucial this is for her business and in general, so now there are regular times when Lisa facilitates freethinking innovation tasks and exercises. They all enjoy this and it has led to some great new ideas. The supplier problem that cropped up is something they've now resolved through having more streamlined processes in place, which weren't there before.

Lisa is getting better at listening. She understands that she can quickly jump to conclusions sometimes so tries to slow down a bit when talking to people, especially competitors. Part of this is also because she has never felt hugely secure setting up her business without a lot of knowledge of the industry, so, consequently, when she meets competitors, she knows that initially she might feel a bit threatened and she now uses this awareness to ask more questions.

Lisa still keeps erratic hours, but these days she is more relaxed and enjoys the evening events more. And when she gets home she tries to wind down before sleeping, which means no iPad in bed!

Critical thinking skills can make a huge difference, as we can see from Lisa's life. Many of us are living like Lisa, flitting from thing to thing and stuffing as much as possible into our days. We can be so much more efficient, creative and effective in our work and in our personal lives if we practise and build critical thinking skills into our day-to-day routines.

Interested in reading more?

Diamond, A. Barnett, W.S., Thomas, J. and Munro, S. (2007) 'Preschool program improves cognitive control', *Science*, 381:1387–88

Elder, L. and Paul, R. (2012) *30 Days to Better Thinking and Better Living with Critical Thinking: A Guide for Improving Every Aspect of Your Life*. Pearson Education

Gathercole, S. and Alloway, T. (2008) *Working Memory and Learning: A Practical Guide for Teachers*. Sage Publications

Goldberg (2001) 'Building the brain's "Air Traffic Control" system: How early experiences shape the development of exective function', National Scientific Council on the Developing Child. Harvard University

Kuncel, N. and Hezlett, S. (2010) 'Fact and fiction in cognitive ability testing for admissions and hiring decisions', *Current Directions in Psychological Science*, 19: 339–45

Winner, M.G. and Crooke, P. (2010) *You Are a Social Detective: Explaining Social Thinking to Kids*. North River Press

www.criticalthinking.org

www.thinkwatson.com

You can also find more tips, ideas and exercises by visiting www.the-advantage.info

Empathy has been proven to be essential for enhancing our interpersonal relationships, overall life satisfaction and improving our ability to cope. But what is empathy exactly? This word originally was coined from the German *einfuehlungsvermogen*. Literally translated, this means being able to feel what another person is feeling. Empathy is the ability to imagine yourself in someone else's position, to identify and understand another's situation, feelings and motives. Perhaps on first glance all this sounds a bit woolly.

What is empathy?

Empathy is often confused with sympathy and, therefore, being sympathetic is often misunderstood as being a key skill or quality we need to and can develop. Empathy is different from sympathy. Sympathy reflects understanding of another person's situation – but viewed through your own lens or perspective. That is, it's based on your version of what the other person is dealing with. An example of this is if a friend has just told you that someone close to them has died. You want to respond genuinely and you can sympathise because, perhaps, you also lost someone close to you a few years back and you dealt with it in a particular way. That may appear to be empathy but you're really only expressing it from your own perspective. Sympathy is actually a form of judgement! Worse, you are probably not even listening actively if you are that ready to come in with your own story. In contrast, empathy is what you feel only when you can step outside of yourself and enter the internal world of the

_____

sympathy is not the same as empathy

_____

other person. There, while still keeping your own perspective, you can experience the other's emotions, conflicts, or aspirations from within the vantage point of that person's world. Really listening, therefore, is an important component of empathy.

Daniel Pink argues in his book *A Whole New Mind*, that empathy is one of six areas **vital** to success today. This is, he says, because empathy is a right-brain (interpersonal) quality and there are three key forces that are now driving the push towards stronger interpersonal skills. He calls them the three As: 'Abundance' is an increasing demand for varied products and services that are aesthetically pleasing; 'Asia' refers to outsourcing; and 'Automation', which, as we know, is happening across all industries. In this environment, the one thing that can't be outsourced or automated is an understanding of what makes others tick, creating trust and strong relationships and generally being caring of others. This is a skill that will become increasingly important in our professional and private lives. It is, if you like, our personal and professional competitive advantage. The skill of empathy can make you really stand out in a company, among individuals in a crowded and noisy marketplace.

Apparently, 1 in 20 of us is a natural born empath, highly adept at being able to read and understand people and resonate with them on many levels. Ginny Whitelaw, author of *The Zen Leader,* suggests it is the most powerful leadership tool there is! I will explain later why some people may be more naturally empathetic, but the good news is that we can all learn and develop this skill. It is definitely something distinctively human and an inner resource and capability.

Why is empathy important?

Why is empathy something we all need to develop more of, rather than simply be aware of what it is? Well, to begin with, without it you will never have strong listening skills or the ability to truly respect others and really value your relationships. Everything you do is more visible, now, than ever before, including how you communicate and relate to others. Everything you do is also more visible to many more people. We know this because the Internet and globalisation has made it so.

Coupled with that, the increasing use of home hubs, social media forums and the hiding behind emails and 'reply to all', without any thought, has meant that empathy is often missing in everyday human interactions. Part of the problem, of course, is that we live in such a distracting world, where so much is happening that we forget to really focus on the person with whom we are communicating. Even if our intention is to put our technology aside, the very act of doing so means that we miss the vital signs and messages in facial expressions in those first few seconds. Our innate ability to empathise has diminished. So we also need to develop empathy because it is a natural skill that we have started to lose and need to now strengthen.

We are increasingly dependent on technology to communicate. Consequently, this may also mean that there is a new need to develop 'virtual empathy'. Interestingly, Twitter founder, Biz Stone, says that technology cannot replace relationships and people's ability to come together around a common cause, and that social media is actually a huge driver for bringing about positive change.[1] Monis Khan, a writer who features the voices of young leaders in *The Washington Post*, is emphatic that young people are, in fact, mastering the ability to empathise because they share their vulnerabilities and desires openly on Facebook.[2] This new media is redefining the way people characterise each other, so rather than looking at those features in which we have no choice, such as age, gender and perhaps even class, this characterisation is now happening through what we do choose, such as our friends, our work and even our favourite music. This automatically creates a generation of connectedness. In the workplace, technology makes it easier than ever to work, share ideas and be productive, despite physical separation. If, as Salman Rushdie once said 're-describing a world is the necessary first step towards changing it', then how we choose to define ourselves and our surroundings may transform any disconnect between young and old and cross-culturally into a potential opportunity for collaboration and progress.

What is certain is that the virtual work environment demands a new set of interpersonal skills and that empathy will play a key role.

How can empathy help us at work?

In *Wired to Care: How Companies Prosper When They Create Widespread Empathy,* top business strategist Dev Patnaik states that organisations of all kinds can tap into a power each of us already naturally has: empathy, the ability to reach outside of ourselves and connect with other people. When people inside a company develop a shared sense of what's going on in the world, they're able to see new opportunities faster than their competitors because they have the courage to be more innovative and take risks. Where empathy plays a part is because the company is far more focused on sincerely understanding the market in-depth and with empathy, and they're doing this collectively.

A key example, taken from *Wired to Care*, is IBM, which was falling apart in the early 1990s and seemed destined to become obsolete. The new CEO, Leo Gerstner, instigated 'Operation Bear Hug', which was simply sending the top 50 managers out to really listen to customers' concerns and to think about how IBM could help address them. The same listening programme was cascaded down to other managers. 'Operation Bear Hug' revealed some major new opportunities for IBM to help companies leverage the power of the emerging Internet, and this strategy literally turned the whole company around; a whole new product was created with a focus on service, rather than on product.

empathy is the power of active listening

There are numerous studies that link empathy to business results. They include studies that correlate empathy with increased sales, with the performance of the best managers of product development teams and with enhanced performance in an increasingly diverse workforce.

Empathy can drive better business results and help retain talent. In a Hay/McBer study of 38,000 leaders and their organisations, leadership styles that rely heavily on empathy are shown to create a more positive company culture and achieve greater bottom-line results.[3] The main thing that these leaders are doing that makes the key difference is actually quite simple: employees feel more comfortable with contributing new ideas and these not being rejected because they are being listened to and they feel valued.

We now see terms such as 'empathy marketing' and 'empathy selling'. Empathy drives marketing because it starts with understanding what people want from you and being able to step into the customers' shoes. Empathy drives sales because the successful salesperson listens first, makes sure they understand what the customer wants and then either delivers on that or helps them find what they are looking for elsewhere. Empathy drives product development because the best kinds of product start with understanding a need and then going from that need. This may all seem really really obvious, but all too often people sell what they *think* the customer wants, rather than giving them what they *actually* want.

Dr Daniel Goleman is a leading psychologist and expert on emotional intelligence (EQ – emotional quotient). Self-awareness is the cornerstone of EQ. You cannot change your IQ, says Goleman, but the good news, he says, is that you can change your emotional intelligence. You can develop it. There is plenty of research that supports this. Emotional intelligence has to do with one's capacity, which is not fixed and tends to grow. It grows through experience, openness and a willingness to learn and be more self-aware. And anyone with a teenager in the house will be very grateful that emotional intelligence does develop!

We live in an age of young, independent, highly marketable and mobile workers. In a popular *Harvard Business Review* article, 'What Makes a Leader', Goleman isolates three reasons why empathy plays such an important role, particularly now:

1 The increasing use of teams, both virtual and face-to-face – even though the patterns of how we work are changing, we do not work in isolation and, in fact, are increasingly dependent on working in all kinds of different types of teams.

2 The rapid pace of globalisation – the increase in cross-cultural communication easily leads to misunderstandings. A 2012 survey by Ernst & Young points to surprisingly big gaps when it comes to cultural knowledge.[4]

3 The growing need to retain talent – key skills are becoming scarcer as baby boomers near retirement age, and the war for talent is getting fiercer because it is harder to find employees with the right skill set. So this means looking after and nurturing the people you have who are good at what they do.

'Leaders with empathy', states Goleman, 'use their knowledge to improve their companies in subtle but important ways.' This doesn't mean that they agree with everyone's view or try to please everybody. Rather, they 'thoughtfully consider employees' feelings – along with other factors – in the process of making intelligent decisions'.

To analyse that further, what employees feel is a result of what they are experiencing in the workplace. The quality of our lives is determined by whether the feelings we have on a day-to-day basis are primarily positive or negative. Positive feelings result in us feeling good, and when that's the case we tend to perform better and contribute actively. It's common sense that feelings influence behaviour and results. So it's good business practice to consider employees' and colleagues' feelings and to seek to make them 'the best that they can be'. Consciously practising the skills of empathy has to be part of that. Unfortunately, considering others' feelings in the workplace can be perceived as being a bit 'wishy-washy' or 'woolly'.

like it or not, it's all about feelings!

Empathy is also referred to as 'social intelligence'. Socially intelligent people are able to assess quickly the emotions of those around them and adapt their words, tone and gestures accordingly. This has always been a key skill for managers and leaders who need to collaborate and build relationships of trust, but now it is even more important for all of us, as we are called upon to collaborate with larger groups of people in different settings, virtual and non-virtual. Our social IQ will continue to be a vital asset. Social IQ is built into the human psyche to greater or lesser degrees and is something that can be developed. In a truly globally connected world, your skill set could see you posted in any number of locations or have work colleagues from very different backgrounds. You will need to be able to operate in whatever environment or cultural context you find yourself. This demands specific abilities, such as language skills, but also an ability to adapt to, sense and respond to changing circumstances and new contexts. Cross-cultural competency will become an important skill for all workers, not just those who have to operate in diverse geographical environments.

Stop and think!

Organisations now increasingly also see diversity as a key driver of innovation.[5] Why is innovation so important? In this market environment, innovation can improve productivity, build brand value, establish new partnerships and relationships and increase turnover and profitability. Businesses that fail to innovate run the very real risk of losing market share to those competitors who are innovating, suffering from falling productivity and efficiency, losing key staff and experiencing steadily reducing margins and profit. No wonder it is prized!

Empathy and social media

The Internet has changed the way we communicate. But being successful on the Internet also requires empathy. A good example of this is online dating sites. I met my husband online and we corresponded for a long time before actually meeting each other. What initially caught my eye was not his picture but how he 'listened' to what I was saying, rather than just telling me how wonderful he is (which he is).

Billy Cripe, the founder of BloomThink, a social media and mobile strategy consultancy, is adamant that using social media to engage well with others relies on empathy. Social media is now used widely as a marketing tool. Successful use of social media correctly anticipates what a customer wants and provides content or product that is interesting and relevant, and precisely aligned to needs. That requires attention and focus – active listening. Honing empathy skills helps you to understand what market needs are and what is relevant content that fits the specific context. Empathy, in this case, makes your listening and your focus that much sharper. I never used Twitter until relatively recently. It has opened up a whole new world and propelled me into much more finely tuned social media empathy skills. It also forces me to respond and, where necessary, change a particular approach. Uncomfortable sometimes? Time-consuming? Yes, but completely necessary if I want to stay one step ahead.

You will also find that your mind and your behaviour patterns adapt and become default mechanisms. So what may, at first, seem like very hard work soon becomes just part of what you do.

Empathy online is important because, unlike other communication channels, with the Internet all the power is placed in the hands of the audience and not the speaker![6] In social media, the target audience will gravitate towards exactly what they want, the way that they want it. They find the product or service rather than the other way round. Empathy with this target audience is key. That means listening to them and being able to put yourself in their shoes, rather than first putting your effort into selling your product or service.

More important now? You bet – because social media not only sharpens the breadth of information we receive but gives all of us a far stronger and easier way to make quick choices. The use of social media in business is growing faster and faster as many come to recognise it as a powerful tool to build brand awareness but also, and this is the most important of all, create strong relationships.

Twitter is becoming the fastest medium for business and Twitter success relies not on selling, but sharing something interesting and relevant and by listening and understanding needs and different perspectives intimately. The ultimate aim is to create that strong relationship and credibility and then to sell. This takes time. And empathy!

empathy – not just touchy-feely but a must-have business skill

Barriers to empathy

All this may well be easier said than done, though – the fact is that, generally, we do not think, see or perceive the world as other people do but we do spend a lot of our time operating within our own way of thinking, seeing or perceiving the world and expecting everyone else to be operating from the same paradigm. This is a waste of time, since they don't and they can't. However, practising empathy consistently across a variety of interpersonal situations in the course of our day requires work and a conscious degree of attention, as well as real effort.

Understanding context

One of the challenges with empathy is that seemingly similar situations can still be very different because the surrounding details and specific circumstances may vary, and the way people deal with experiences varies greatly as well. For example, two people who have just lost their jobs will have two completely different experiences and responses. Person A loses their job and reacts with anger and disbelief, as well as feeling debilitated (due to factors such as their perception of their age, type of work and their self-belief – perhaps they also have a large family and no savings). Person B loses their job and experiences great sadness and worry but at the same time is excited, although scared, about the new opportunities this represents (due to other factors – maybe they have a dream they have always wanted to pursue and can more easily pursue it as they have savings and no family, for example). Alternatively, they may naturally respond to change in a different way – see the chapter on resilience.

Stop and think!

If you are discussing a friend's personal situation, you are very likely also to be looking at it from your own perspective - i.e. how YOU would feel if YOU lost your job - making true empathy harder still.

The things that are unsaid

We also need to be more aware of what is not being said or expressed, or concealed behind niceties. Empathy has to get right behind 'polite' behaviour and be able to bring sometimes uncomfortable issues out into the open. That means empathy works with information that is as accurate as it can be. That's done through careful listening, and the more willing you are to understand someone else's perspective, the more accurate the information they give you will be. How do you do that? By asking the right kinds of open questions and observing body language. If your goal is to lead or influence someone, the first consideration must be to your own personal behaviour. Most people absolutely do not listen with the intent to understand; most people are preparing to speak when their turn comes next. I know because I catch myself doing it numerous times a day. Empathy takes effort and conscientiousness.

Stop and think!

When you actively listen you can literally transform the conversation you are having. And, because others don't often experience the gift of listening, when you take the time and attention to listen to them, they perceive this (and you) in a highly positive way. It's so simple really! But something that we find hard to do day-to-day and consistently.

So, empathy is not only about really understanding someone's feelings and thoughts but also understanding real constraints and pressures that may not be revealed in an initial verbal exchange. An example of this is in a negotiation situation, where it's important to understand the objectives and constraints that underlie the discussion, both at the corporate level and the personal level. This requires wider discussion and research around the immediate issue being negotiated.

The ego

Our strongly developed sense of individuality – or being a personal self, or ego – can make it difficult for us to experience this state of connection. The ego 'walls us off' from other people. We spend most of our day walking around focused on ourselves and looking at everything from our own perspective. This is completely natural and is probably heightened by our increasing propensity to react rather than respond to events around us. Therefore, empathy requires effort on our part, at least initially to kick it back into gear.

Recent studies in the USA show that students have 40 per cent *less* empathy than 30 years ago.[7] Reasons for this are said to be societal changes – i.e. violence in the media, modern technology, video games and the rise of social media generally, which has reduced face-to-face interaction. Compare this, though, with what was said earlier about how social media influences empathy for the better and you have another way of looking at it all. Add to this a generally hyper-competitive atmosphere, with inflated expectations of success borne of celebrity reality shows, and you have a very complex environment in which to encourage the importance of building empathy.

> managing and nurturing all your relationships, both online and face to face, is and will continue to be a key skill and competence

Can we develop empathy?

Some people are naturally good at empathy. Neuroscience suggests that empathy is connected with how our brains work.[8] So, although this means that some people may well be better at it than others, it also means that it can be learned. According to neuroscientist Dr Shanida Nataraja, Westerners use the left hemisphere of their brain too much, focusing on the logical, rational and analytical aspects of the mind. Why do we use this side too much? Well, partly because of the world we live in and its overload of information, and the brain processing required to handle it.

The right hemisphere of the brain is associated with seeing the whole picture, emotional expression, creativity, non-verbal awareness and visual and spatial perception, and it is the neural site of empathy. In fact, considerable research shows that the capacity to feel what another person feels is hard-wired through what are called 'mirror neurons', which connect your brain like Wi-Fi with people you observe.[9] Functional magnetic resonance imagery (fMRI) shows that regions of the brain involving both emotions and physical sensations light up in someone who observes or becomes aware of another person's pain or distress.[10] Literally, you do feel another's pain or other emotions. Similar research[11] shows that generosity and altruistic behaviour light up pleasure centres of the brain usually associated with food or sex.[12]

When you walk down the street and someone comes your way, it's likely you will both move in the same direction, even though you are trying to get out of each other's way. This is because your mirror neurons sensed the person's intentions and you 'mirrored' their actions until your cognitive brain could engineer an opposing move that cleared the path.[13] These mirror neurons enable us to experience empathy and show that, to a greater or lesser extent, we are each in fact hard-wired to be empathetic.

'One develops a moral sensitivity to the extent one is embedded, from infancy, in a nurturing parental, familial, and neighborhood environment. Society can foster that environment by providing the appropriate social and public context. While primitive empathic potential is wired into the brain chemistry of some mammals, and especially the primates, its mature expression in humans requires learning and practice and a conducive environment.'

Jeremy Rifkin, author of *The Empathic Civilization*

This suggests empathy is a skill that needs to be mastered.

So, how do we become more empathetic?

One of the problems with most articles and books about empathy is that they are either rather vague, or highly demanding in the techniques they suggest. There are certain things we can start out by being more aware of, and pay more attention to these in our daily interactions with others.

Reading faces

According to Daniel Pink's book *A Whole New Mind*, we need to start by being better at reading people's faces and body language, so that means paying far more attention to people we are interacting with than we normally do.[14] This is because facial expressions that demonstrate the real feelings underneath, which are not being voiced, are visible only for a few seconds (Paul Ekman in *Emotions Revealed*,[15]) but long enough to recognise easily if you are paying attention and are not distracted by your own thoughts. He says that what we need to begin to understand are the micro-expressions within these, which are there for an even briefer time.

Active listening

We can also practise far more active listening. This is a skill that, although hard work, can be put into practice in virtually any situation with immediate effect.

There are four kinds of listening and you will easily recognise these because either you've been on the receiving end of them or you do it yourself:

- Pretending to listen – 'yeah, uh huh, right'
- Selective – tuning in and out
- Attentive – paying attention to the words being said so that you can repeat them, but not necessarily understanding the message
- Empathic – listening with the intent to understand, and that is active listening.

Because we tend to listen autobiographically most of the time, we are likely to respond in one of four typical ways, when others tell us something:

1 We **evaluate** – we decide if we agree or disagree, as in 'do you really believe that?'

2 We **probe** – asking questions to clarify, e.g. 'What's wrong?'

3 We **advise** – giving counsel based on our personal experience: 'give it some time, it will be OK'.

4 We **interpret** – we try to explain others' behaviours and motives: 'you're just angry now, it'll be fine later on'.

Active listening cuts across all of this, but it does mean putting these natural reactive responses to one side.

Here are two key components of active listening:

Being interested in what the other person is saying, with a readiness and ability to listen. Now, we may not actually *be* interested initially but, curiously, by acting interested we start to become interested. How do you show interest? By everything from body language to reflecting back to the other person what is being said in what we say or write.

Being present. Most of the time, when others are speaking, we are focused on what we are going to say next or on our own thoughts, and are less likely to be anchored in the present moment. We may have to force ourselves to be present, but when we are it pays huge dividends.

So, the next time you communicate with anyone, set aside your own need to say the next thing and genuinely seek to understand. Don't push, be patient, be respectful, understand their emotions, clarify their statements and be discerning, sensitive and aware.

Just try it next time you are talking with your partner or spouse. Then try it at work. You will see an immediate

want to be liked? all you have to do is listen!

change, either in the direction your conversation takes or the outcome as a result of that conversation.

Total immersion

Another way to develop empathy is to try to totally and completely immerse ourselves in what it might feel like to walk in another person's shoes. This is hard to do because it means consciously directing our awareness to something our mind does not naturally gravitate towards. That's because our sense of individuality and ego is so very strong and ingrained. However, it is possible. It's possible through consciously focusing on another person and stepping outside of ourselves; through really listening and making sure we understand. Most of the time we focus our attention only on ourselves. Every single experience, from standing in line at the bank to attending a meeting, is undertaken through our own personal lens. Try doing this a different way. It's hard work and it's exhausting but it does have an immediate impact. Try practising this focus in an every-day situation and notice the effect it has. An example: you go into your local bank to pay in some money. There's a long queue and you're in a hurry. Finally, you get to the window. Instead of conducting the transaction in a hurry and barely looking at the woman behind the counter, blaming the bank and by default the woman serving you, you smile and ask how she is and maybe even acknowledge the wait. The effect can be transformational. And you will certainly feel a lot happier immediately as a result. That is why customer-centric banks will train their staff to do just this, so it's you on the receiving end.

Why is empathy that powerful? Psychologically, empathy is crucial as it meets the critical human need of personal affirmation. After physical survival, the greatest need of a human being is psychological survival – to be understood, to be affirmed, to be validated and to be appreciated. So when you listen empathically, you are giving that person psychological affirmation of their value as a person. That is why it works every time.

Building self-awareness and focus

Apart from learning how to read faces, active listening and immersing ourselves, there are other key elements of empathy that we should be focusing on. These are self-awareness, non-judgement and self-confidence. These are the subsets of skills we can develop in training to help build empathy. And the ways of doing this?

Forum theatre

One fantastic technique, which could be used more in mainstream education and training, is forum theatre.[16] This is a hugely successful tool to help understand others' perspectives through empathy – a low-risk, high-gain opportunity to walk around in others' shoes and explore language and behaviour. It works because the actors or audience members can stop a performance, usually a short, scripted scene depicting a conflict and ending on a 'cliff-hanger' where it appears there is no solution. You don't need trained actors for forum theatre, you can use two confident individuals. Once the cliff-hanger is reached, the audience can then 'get to know' the characters by asking them more about themselves and their backgrounds. The audience then suggests different actions for the actors to carry out on-stage in an attempt to change the outcome of what they are seeing. Forum theatre is a stressless investment for learners as they don't have to actually get up and role-play, but they still have a huge level of involvement; or it might allow them to challenge someone's behaviour on another's behalf. Scenes are based on real issues that have been given a dramatic context to bring out discussion.

Mindfulness meditation

One way to activate right-brain thinking, which I referred to earlier as the hardwire key to interpersonal skills and empathy, is by practising mindfulness meditation, defined as a heightened awareness of the present moment that comes about by observing thought patterns and emotion without judgement or getting overly involved.[17] This has been shown to create significant changes in the areas of the brain connected to attention and feelings. This kind of meditation results in an increased ability to focus, as well as to reflect and relax. But, most importantly, it strengthens the right brain, which unlocks your hardwired empathy abilities.

> mindfulness meditation is on the increase in the workplace

Think this is not something business people could get into? Penelope Mavor, a leadership consultant, says:

> *'I think increasingly there are people who are curious to develop these skills and are being trained and coached to do so, such as the pharmacists I will be working with this week in Riga. One "technique" I will be emphasising with them, as a way to develop empathy, is learning to quiet our own inner state. Through practising mindfulness, such as bringing our awareness and attention to the present by noticing our breathing, the greater chance we have of connecting with ourselves and with others in the moment.'*

Perhaps it helps to consider a definition of mind**less**ness to highlight how being mind**ful** can help with empathy.

Mindlessness involves automatic, habitual thought. That means you treat information as though it is context-free and true, regardless of circumstances. Mindlessness is most common when people are distracted, hurried, multi-tasking or overloaded.[18] Since people are hurrying, multi-tasking and feeling overloaded most of the time, we need to attack our default pattern of mindlessness.

There are now increasingly more examples of mindfulness being practised at work. A recent Twitter search at the time of writing this text brought up several examples, including:

- A study done by the University of Washington, which found that a group of HR managers who were given meditation and Zen mindfulness training were able to stay on task longer, be more focused and be less distracted.[19] A positive side effect was that they were also less stressed.

- The first UK 'Mindfulness at Work' Conference, which took place in 2012, featuring many seminars and workshops on increasing employee resilience, productivity and communication skills.

- Several 'mindfulness at work' training programmes, tailored specifically for the workplace to encourage adaptability, flexibility and self-awareness.

And outside of work, how about that Yoga or Pilates class? According to neuropsychologist Dr Rick Hanson, when you focus on your body and breathing, whether through meditation or something like Pilates, dance or Yoga, the area of the brain known as the insular cortex actually thickens; this is the part of the brain to do with the internal state of the body and gut feelings and the emotional state of other people.[20]

So, by incorporating some of these into our daily lives, our innate ability to empathise will become stronger. It's a bit like exercising a muscle.

Neuro-linguistic programming (NLP)

Neuro-linguistic programming (NLP) is an approach to communication, personal development and psychotherapy created in the 1970s and refers to a connection between neurological processes ('neuro'), language ('linguistic') and behavioural patterns learned through experience ('programming'). Although many neuroscientists, psychologists and linguists say that NLP is unsupported by current scientific evidence, I mention it here because it is used widely for developing empathy and helping to understand how other people process information using various stages.[21] One of

NLP's stages is about developing rapport and understanding non-verbal cues and facial expressions. Active listening is also used widely in NLP. Whether or not one agrees with NLP as a science, these techniques can help support the development of empathy.

The advantage of NLP-related techniques for creating rapport is that they are short and simple and don't require a person to be tracking half-a-dozen kinds of signals at the same time as they are trying to understand what the other person is saying. The main techniques used in NLP for establishing rapport, or supporting empathy, are where you match and mirror someone's body language as well as the type of language they are using. Basically, by matching and mirroring them you are becoming more like them and, therefore, able to get a better understanding of their world.

Matching and mirroring body language

Any observable behaviour can be mirrored. This includes body posture, hand gestures, head tilt, facial expression, energy level, breathing rate and vocal qualities (volume, tone, rhythm). Ever noticed, in a meeting that is going well, everyone ends up sitting in the same way? Quite often, if empathy is being achieved in a meeting or conversation, you will notice a completely natural mirroring going on with no conscious effort made to do so. You can turn this on its head and contribute significantly towards a favourable outcome by subtly mirroring body language. Just make sure you're actively listening as well, though!

Matching and mirroring verbal language

This is achieved by paying close attention to the words, phrases and images someone uses when they are speaking. What someone is saying may be the same semantically, but involves different processes:

- **Visual:** words used – 'I see what you mean', 'This idea looks good to me', 'I want the big picture', 'Let's focus on the details later'.

- **Auditory:** words used – 'Tell me again... I'm not sure I heard you right', 'That sounds like a good idea', 'Let me use you as a sounding board...', 'Yes, that's as clear as a bell'.

- **Feeling:** words used – 'I sense what you mean', 'That idea feels right', 'I can't get a handle on this concept', 'He's the kind of person who can take an idea and run with it'.

Although we probably use a mix of these, there will usually be a dominant pattern. If the other person is using mainly 'visual' words, so should you. This may feel uncomfortable, possibly even mildly manipulative at first, but the thinking is that it supports the development of rapport and helps to create empathy.

10 steps to empathy

Here are some simple steps to help you improve your empathy skills. Try these out in your next meeting or your next conversation. See what happens. Try and keep a record of what took place when you consciously focused on empathy.

1 **Take note of situations in which you demonstrated empathy**
   What was happening? Think about things that were going on for you immediately leading up to that specific situation and what contributed to you demonstrating empathy. Think about how you felt at the time – for example, if you were feeling optimistic and not distracted, maybe this had an impact on how able you were to show empathy. Maybe you were focused on active listening, which changed the results of that situation for the better.

2 **What happens when there's no empathy?**
   Think about a time when you were less able to show empathy. Can you remember times when other people's underlying concerns were not explicitly expressed and/or addressed? Why did this happen? What triggered this? The more you

are aware of this, the more you can pre-empt this happening in the future. Sometimes empathy is the hardest to express with those closest to us, such as our spouse, partner or child. That's because we are so often caught up in our own priorities, thoughts or feelings. Don't take the people closest to you for granted (see also step number 9: the Pygmalion effect).

3 Start listening!

Practise listening without interrupting or judging. Use some of the active listening described in this chapter. Try simple things such as waiting until others fully express their points of view before offering your own (hard to do at first!). Try it the very next time you have a conversation with someone. Note the result or impact.

4 Start looking after yourself

Become more aware of any stress factors in your day. These may tend to happen at a particular time of day, when you are juggling tasks or when you've had a demanding time at work. If you know when you are prone to stress, take care of this by building in time for yourself, or reflection space. Choose your times for listening and put stress to one side. This can only happen if you are taking responsibility for managing this. Choose your responses!

5 Slow down

Build in reflection time and mindfulness into your day as much as you can. If you are constantly rushing from one stimulus to the other, you are far less likely to be empathetic to others. Explore mindfulness. If nothing else, just try being still and silent for a short time and breathe deeply. This can be done while waiting for a train, instead of automatically pulling out your smartphone.

6 Practise, practise, practise!

If there is someone in your life with whom you have difficulty communicating, consciously try and identify what emotions they may be experiencing when interacting with you. Explore the possibilities without assuming that what you identify is necessarily true. Develop a list of questions for your next encounter with this person. What sort of questions would you ask now that could help increase your understanding and create a better conversation or outcome?

7 **Get better at reading faces and body language**
This is something we probably don't ever consciously focus on. But try it. Really pay attention to facial expression and body language the next time you are in a meeting or discussion. What is happening? How sensitive are you to non-verbal cues? Look at someone's face for that very first initial response, which is so hard to disguise!

8 **Think about outcomes**
So often we focus on outcomes but in the wrong way because we don't focus on the behaviour required to reach that outcome. For example, let's say my outcome is to have an enjoyable evening with my husband at the theatre. Well, that actually starts with how we interact with each other within minutes of meeting up after work. If my mood is negative or reactive, it will definitely result in defensive or irrational behaviour of sorts on my part, which will impact the whole evening. Another way is to actually change the desired outcome to focus instead on the other person. My desired outcome, then, is for my husband to have a wonderful and enjoyable evening. Just by stating that and writing it down, I am more likely to engage in behaviour that will lead to this positive outcome.

9 **Beware of the Pygmalion effect**[22]
How you view someone persistently that you closely interact with can have an effect on how they perform – a self-fulfilling prophecy. People are very good at sensing how we view them. We translate this through a multitude of micro-gestures: frequently checking email while they talk to us, picking up the phone when they enter our office, or looking away when they are talking. All of these seemingly insignificant gestures

are posters with a clear message: you are not important. Put yourself in their shoes for a moment and try to experience what that must feel like. Developing empathy involves putting our foot on the brake for a moment to think about these things and how they might be coming across to others.

10 Start cultivating 'social generosity'

Also known as 'executive presence', this means that people walk away from you feeling energised and better about themselves and not the opposite, which is feeling drained! So help others to feel important, always see them as who they can become, the best of themselves. This connection can't happen without empathy. So pay attention, say positive things and listen when you talk to other people. Do this in small ways with family and friends and then at work for noticeable effect.

A day in the life of...

Let's take a magnifying glass to the skill of empathy through a day in the life of Jan. We'll start with a brief introduction to Jan, to give a quick snapshot of his life.

About Jan

Jan is a manager in his early forties. He's got an engineering background and is now responsible for health and safety compliance in an oil company. Jan is extremely hard-working and ambitious and wants to get on in his career. He knows this is the optimum time to get a prime senior position in the company. He works long hours and has a young family. His wife doesn't work and is at home with the children. Jan commutes to his work in the city from the suburbs. He is highly methodical and logical, working to clear structures and routines.

At the moment Jan is pondering what to do about his recent 360-degree feedback exercise results. Overall, the feedback about his performance from colleagues, staff and his boss has been excellent. He expects total professionalism, dedication and hard work from his team. However, his scores on empathy have been fairly low in comparison and there have been qualitative comments such as 'he never fully listens to our point of view', 'he expects us to work excessive hours and we can't see the point', 'he's completely intolerant when we make mistakes', 'he doesn't cut any slack' and 'team performance is suffering'.

Actually the feedback doesn't come as a total surprise to Jan, as he is aware that for some reason he doesn't empathise with others. His wife has made similar comments. He generally thinks that listening and considering employees' feelings is a bit out of touch with pushing ahead with work, and he doesn't have that much tolerance for anyone whom he perceives as not putting in as much effort as he does. He can see that his management style may be impacting on his team performance and also may be an impediment to his advancement within the company. Jan is doing well and should get promoted fairly soon.

Let's have a closer look at a typical day in Jan's life and how building the skill of empathy can help him.

Jan's typical day

When Jan's in the office he gets up at 7am and takes a bus or taxi to work. He has a healthy breakfast of porridge and fresh fruit and black coffee. Today he has meetings with his team almost all day, with a short break for a working lunch. At least one week in every month he travels to overseas locations to meet the other teams engaged on offshore projects. He really enjoys his work. Most of the time he is home by 7pm each evening and has dinner with his wife. Jan is lean and fit and *enjoys cycling and tennis in his free time. Today he gets home feeling a bit irritable and argues with his wife – mainly because she wants to talk to him about her day with the kids. This sort of argument is becoming more frequent, and neither Jan nor his wife are addressing the arguments at the moment. He's a bit preoccupied today, anyway, about his 360-degree feedback results. He is actually a bit upset by the comments and puzzled too, as he thinks everyone should be more driven these days and he thinks he communicates quite well, even if he is a bit abrupt at times.*

Jan genuinely enjoys his work.

What's going on here?

Jan is fairly typical of managers with a strong technical background who encounter issues with their management style in more senior roles. They are highly logical and use this logic to good effect in their decision making. They do, however, often lack empathy, or at least the ability to display empathy. In many technical occupations this may not be an issue, but certainly becomes more of an issue when interacting with other people. There are several elements to consider here. Although empathetic skills are developable to some extent, Jan will also need to desire to change, as such development requires hard work and commitment. Jan may also feel that if he goes 'soft' he may lose his cutting edge. In Jan's case he can logically see the benefits of becoming more empathetic as it will improve team performance and his own promotion prospects. He is unlikely to be promoted if he is unable to lead his team effectively, and the perception he is giving is that he isn't. There is nothing wrong with demanding professionalism and dedication, as well as hard work, but if he were leading well, then his team would want to go that extra bit further and work longer hours, etc. It may well be that in his case he will never be able to BE empathetic in the sense that he can truly put himself in someone else's shoes. However, with support, he could use his highly developed logic to understand how his staff may react to his behaviour and modify his own behaviour accordingly.

One day, Jan watches a debate about why we need to develop our inner resources more strongly. He's intrigued because he agrees with the idea that people should be more self-reliant. He decides to start focusing more on his empathy skills.

Let's revisit Jan's 'typical day' six months later.

How Jan's life has moved forward

Jan's increasingly regular arguments with his wife, combined with his recent 360-degree feedback, propelled him to want to make some changes. His first step was to keep a daily log and note down situations at work where his style of interaction with colleagues might be leading to reduced performance in the team. For example, he asked a colleague when the quality standards on the Nigerian oilfield will be completed. His colleague said it was slightly behind schedule because of illness in one of the team members. Jan displayed his annoyance and irritation but caught himself just in time to try and tone it down a bit. He then used a coach to help him look at alternative strategies of dealing with this kind of situation. The coach helped Jan look at questions he could have asked, before reacting, that would have helped him understand the true nature of this issue – i.e., is it really about resources and team members or more about the fact that the team did not feel comfortable telling him there was an illness in the first place? This helped Jan see that, in fact, it was his responsibility to ensure that deadlines are being met and that the team have the required resources to deliver.

Jan started to practise more active listening skills. He knew that the first ten minutes of coming home were probably the most important in terms of determining how the evening might go. Although he did not find it easy at first, his logic enabled him to recognise immediately his natural default way of 'listening', so he tried very small things such as asking his wife more questions about her day and not jumping in with his own immediate responses. Jan also recognised that by not demonstrating empathy skills at work, he was becoming someone that people were starting not to like, which was a shock in a way but also a wake-up call to raising his self-awareness. He's started to think first before responding and to try to deploy the same active listening skills at work, since it had such an immediate impact on his relationship.

Jan thinks about outcomes more and how to ensure those are reached through being more aware of his own behaviour. Snapping at work colleagues does not create an outcome of a positive, efficient team – when Jan looks at it logically from this perspective it all makes a lot more sense. The team are, in fact, quite driven, like Jan is, but now they feel part of a real team. Jan now tends not to just tell people what to do but spends time explaining what and why, and talking through things in such a way as to get the team's views. They feel they are being listened to and Jan is able to get more out of them as a result. Jan gets their views but, being their boss, makes decisions that may or may not accommodate the team's views.

Jan will likely never be naturally empathetic, but by using his logic he is able to move beyond seeing empathy as something 'touchy-feely' and 'soft' to something that he requires to move ahead. He also notices that his own behaviour has a much greater impact on others than he realises, and that this can be either negative or positive depending on how he approaches a situation. He is also creating stronger relationships and it is these that will help him to move forward in his career. In fact,

*being promoted and achieving a more senior role is largely
down to his empathy skills.*

Empathy is not about being 'soft' or sympathetic, as we now
know. It can help us to develop successful and dynamic work
and personal relationships. And those relationships are really
our only true sources of competitive advantage or distinction.
Empathy, perhaps more than any other skill, is the most
challenging to develop as our natural instinct to focus only on
ourselves is very strong.

Interested in reading more?

Chaskalson, M. (2011) *The Mindful Workplace: Developing Resilient Individuals and Resonant Organizations with MBSR.* Wiley-Blackwell

Ekman, P. (2004) *Emotions Revealed: Understanding Faces and Feelings.* Phoenix

Goleman, D. (2004) *Emotional Intelligence and Working with Emotional Intelligence, Working with EQ.* Bloomsbury Publishing

Goleman, D. (1998) 'What makes a leader?' *Harvard Business Review*

Patnaik, D. (2009) *Wired to Care: How Companies Prosper When They Create Widespread Empathy.* Prentice Hall

Pink, D. (2008) *A Whole New Mind: Why Right-Brainers Will Rule the Future.* Marshall Cavendish

Rifkin, Jeremy (2010) *The Empathic Civilization.* Polity Press

Whitelaw, G. (2012) *The Zen Leader: 10 Ways to go from Barely Managing to Leading Fearlessly.* Career Press

You can also find more tips, ideas and exercises by visiting www.the-advantage.info

'If you have integrity, nothing else matters. If you don't have integrity, nothing else matters.'

Alan K. Simpson

Chapter 4

INTEGRITY

'Empathy is trying on someone else's shoes – sympathy is wearing them.'

Unknown

Chapter 3

EMPATHY

ntegrity is not straightforward to define and will vary from person to person. You can think of it like a moral compass, holding true to your values and beliefs, and in many ways integrity is about character. It is what you do when no one else is looking, and all depends on a combination of the following: specific circumstances, what we believe to be right, our values and how we choose to conduct ourselves. For instance, is integrity about little things such as following through on a promise, or big things like not fiddling your expenses? Or is fiddling your expenses a little thing and not following through on a promise a big thing?

What is integrity?

Integrity can be defined as 'integrated', meaning congruent words, actions and thoughts and, therefore, congruence between what you say and what you do. In plain English, this is about walking the talk. If we include values in this then even thieves have values, so holding true to them – is that integrity? Or is it more about principles? In fact, integrity is connected with both values and principles.

First of all, we need to make a distinction between principles and values as these are often interchanged. Both principles and values are generally the rules of life that each of us chooses to live by. Principles are about the expected behaviour of a society, and these in turn have a collective influence on everyone. So principles might include concepts such as fairness, justice, diligence, honesty, compassion and even how we define integrity. Principles are different depending on the society or culture.

Values, though, are personal, subjective ideals, beliefs and individual traits that a person can feel affinity with and are not related to principles or standards. They may also change over time. Values can include concepts such as freedom, security, power, creativity and adventure. How those values, in turn, are interpreted will also vary from individual to individual. After all, adventure could be defined as anything from a bungee jump to a love of travel or risky behaviour, which may have negative consequences.

> principles provide anchors and a sense of internal balance and values help us to develop our potential

Values and principles are important because awareness of these helps you to understand who you are. If integrity is about being true to yourself, having your own 'moral' compass and a strong connection between what you say and your actions, then values and principles will, to a certain extent, define how you express your integrity.

Here is another definition that came from a Twitter discussion:

'Integrity means inwardly doings things that are aligned to your values, outwardly doing things ethically and morally.'

This encourages us to think more deeply and explore the ethics of integrity. We can certainly all think of famous instances where people held strong to their inward values, but their actions were viewed as unethical and immoral. However, values in a society can and do change, and what may have been acceptable at a specific point in time becomes unacceptable, and vice versa.

Back to basics

We need to bring the topic of integrity right back to the significant measure of self-awareness and self-honesty required to be truly consistent and authentic. This, in turn, helps us to strip away agendas that may even be hidden from ourselves, let alone others.

Stephen Carter, in his book *Integrity*, defines integrity as a virtue of character that requires three steps: 1) **discerning** what is right and what is wrong; 2) **acting on** what you have discovered, even at personal cost; and 3) **saying openly** that you are acting on your understanding of right from wrong.[1]

The term 'discerning' refers to being able to make that moral choice between what is right and wrong. This alone is not enough; the second step requires you to act on that knowledge, such as keeping commitments, and the third is being open and taking initiative.

According to the FBI, integrity is 'total commitment to honesty in every aspect of a person's life. Integrity goes to the core of conduct, what people believe in their heart of hearts. It cannot be bought, claimed or bestowed. It does not come with office, title or appointment. It simply exists. The person who has integrity rarely claims it. The person who claims it rarely has it. Integrity is best manifested quietly in day-to-day living and in the workplace. It should be treasured above all things, for after integrity comes decency, honour, trust and principle.'[2]

Integrity can be seen as something that is present and known only to ourselves (what we do when no one else is looking) and something that is also recognised and perceived as highly positive by the external world.

Integrity comes from the Latin word *integer*, which means intact or whole.

So, when we have integrity we:

- are authentic – conducting our lives in a way that is true to our values
- act consistently
- take responsibility and 'own' all of our feelings and behaviours
- do what we say we will do
- hold ourselves accountable

- communicate the truth respectfully and don't leave out important information
- actively listen and seek to understand others' points of view
- are emotionally open, receptive and willing to share our feelings
- don't have hidden agendas.

Why is integrity important?

Isn't integrity subjective and personal and, maybe at the end of the day, simply down to how we behave as individuals? Isn't there lots of room for integrity to be 'faked', or used as a way to justify (just about) any action?

Integrity is a quality, and maybe even an old-fashioned quality we have actually lost sight of. Dr Stephen Covey said in an interview, just before his death, that the economic and global crisis we have recently experienced creates humility because pain humbles people and, because of this, makes them more open and teachable.[3] Dr Covey believed that principle-centred leadership was crucial in a changing and challenging world and that the key to this was understanding moral authority versus formal authority. He said that, 'Moral authority comes from being centred on principles, which are universal and timeless. Principles such as fairness, trust, integrity, compassion and honesty are central to enduring leadership – at work, at home or in the community.'

We tend to associate integrity with leadership because it is about making the right decisions and it embraces ethics and 'doing the right thing'. However, it is becoming increasingly important simply because the world is changing so fast. In the midst of change and stormy waters, integrity can become the very thing that differentiates you and makes you stand out. Of course, lack of integrity can do the same, but in this age of transparency and visibility, combined with heightened uncertainty and rapid change, it will be increasingly important to demonstrate trust, honesty and doing the right thing. Having integrity can make a huge impact when it comes to others being able to trust you. It means that you will be the person they come to, whether it's to confide in you, to support you or give you that much needed break or work opportunity.

Why have we lost sight of integrity? Gary Fenstermacher, Professor Emeritus at the University of Michigan, says that the kind of integrity as exemplified by the likes of Martin Luther King has become eroded in recent history. He says that leaders in multiple sectors of society have failed to exemplify discernment, right action and transparency; that integrity has lost out to pride, self-interest, ambition, greed and pursuit of power.[4] We can certainly point to the global economic crisis and find many examples of this. I would also argue that self-interest, ambition, pursuit of power and so on, are very human traits. We are capable of great integrity, greed and self-interest. Self-interest can lead us to act in ways that are not aligned to integrity and sometimes it is even the easier choice. A very simple example: if I've arranged to go out with a friend but something else comes up that seems more attractive or more urgent (an opportunity to do something else), I might tell the friend I'm not feeling well and cancel our arrangement. This serves my own interests but I know I am not telling the truth. It may be easier to do but inwardly I may feel uneasy or even upset with myself. Not acting in congruence with 'the right thing' will lead to a type of uneasiness within myself, even if I am able to justify my actions, and I won't sleep well at night.

So, we need to understand that, while an action that displays a lack of integrity may seem like the best way to get ahead, it won't work in the longer term. It's more likely to be a one-off gain, which may undermine long-term success when it comes to needing someone's help, or his or her trust. It means that others won't necessarily trust you and, if you have set-backs, you will recover less easily. We can never know the true impact of our actions.

Another example: I agree to give a presentation at a conference because at the time it seemed like an interesting opportunity, and then nearer the time I cancel because I 'have too much on', or just can't be bothered to give the presentation I said I would do. Or some other attractive and paid work comes up, so I take that instead. It all seems quite legitimate and justifiable. But the resulting consequences in the longer term may mean anything from missing out on a potential networking opportunity to the conference organisers knowing one of my key clients and some-how they learn of my cancellation. The advent of social media now means that such ripple effects are even more likely.

Can you be ruthless and have integrity?

Yes. Shakespeare's play *Henry V* proposes that the qualities that define a good leader may not necessarily be the same as the ones that define a good person. Henry is a great leader – intelligent, focused, charismatic and inspiring to others. He also uses any and all resources to ensure he achieves his goals and is actually quite ruthless in doing so. Shakespeare's play focuses on events before and just after the Battle of Agincourt. Henry V acted extremely aggressively and harshly to prevent loss of life on the English side, but this ruthlessness is perfectly aligned with his values in terms of fighting for a belief in a God-given right to hold the French crown and acting in the best interest of the people fighting for him.

Can you be dishonest and have integrity?

Less likely, because integrity is rooted in morals and princi-ples. Stephen Covey said that if there isn't deep integrity within a person, then the challenges of life will, ultimately, cause true motives to rise to the surface. Many people who do achieve strong leadership and strong success socially can actually lack what is needed for integrity. Dig behind the success and you are likely to find this reflected in any longer-term relationship they have, whether that's with a business associate, romantic relationship or a teenage son or daughter going through difficulty. Some say the recent world events are encouraging a return to old-fashioned principles and morals. So, perhaps, there is about to be a U-turn for embracing integrity.

Where to start with integrity

I think integrity begins with small things. The small things tell you a lot about a person. At a very basic level, integrity is about knowing the difference between right and wrong – it's our conscience, if you like. Any action can be justified, though, and what may be wrong to one person may well be right to another. Each person will have their own moral compass. Perhaps to strip this back, integrity is simply about doing what you say you will do, being honest and forthright. Walking your talk. Doing the right thing even when no one is looking.

do sweat the small stuff

As our speed of life has accelerated, so has the number of people who are neglecting to do the things that are expected of them. Being late for appointments, failing to return calls and emails, changing plans at the last minute and not completing projects on time are an everyday occurrence. These may seem like small things but they are not! If I'm honest, I even have to remind myself that actually it is not OK to be late, cancel at short notice or request extensions to deadlines for something I've miscalculated. It's become so easy to do, though, and we are all guilty of it and we all do it.

Integrity is a vital quality in work and life. These days we think nothing of changing something at the last minute, without undue concern about the person we have let down. In fact, you are probably finding that more and more appointments come with a last-minute call or a text or an email announcing a late arrival or a change of plan. And if it's not you sending those texts, you're probably on the receiving end of them. Part of this is, of course, because we can. Our lifestyles and our reliance on technology encourage this. So does our love of what we think is multi-tasking as we hurtle through our lives. Social media and mobile phones are creating a strong tidal pull towards what's known as 'poly-chronic behaviours'.[5] At least two generations have already been taught to process information in this way rather than chrono-logically and in sequence. Our mobile devices are always on, interrupting us with notifications about what others are doing and saying. This forces us to embrace more multi-tasking, more fluidity in our daily activities.

> texting, emailing and watching a film while posting on Facebook is not multi-tasking!

However, multi-tasking is really only possible when two conditions are being met: 1) one of the tasks is so well-learned it is almost automatic and does not require thought or concentration, for example eating or walking; and 2) the tasks involve different kinds of brain pro-cessing. A good example of real multi-tasking is reading a book while listening to classical music, because reading comprehension and listening to music engage different parts of our brain. When you are using the same part of your brain to process information through your laptop, tablet or smartphone your ability to retain that information is actually declining significantly. Your ability to focus your attention is also reduced, which in turn leads to con-stant distractions that have an impact on the way you behave and on the way you treat others.

So what has all this got to do with integrity? Well, it's become so acceptable now to cancel something at short notice or change arrangements that, if you actually are consistent, keep your word and can be trusted to be on time, you stand out. Everything we do now is so much more transparent and visible. Integrity really is our inner guiding compass and has an impact on how we behave and treat others. We are going through a period of intense change in probably every aspect of our lives – consistency, trust, values and honesty are like a harbour in the storm.

Integrity inspires trust and creates trust. Lack of integrity creates mistrust and lowers respect and openness.

Integrity is one constant in our extremely fluid world and it goes where you go. And a bonus: if you are acting in line with what you believe in and know to be right, you will, quite simply, feel happier and less stressed.

> be the harbour in the storm

How can integrity help us at work?

Most companies have integrity baked into their values or mission statements. It's typically worded something like, 'We act with absolute integrity', or 'We build value through integrity...'. Integrity is a powerful but often misunderstood concept. Many define integrity as honesty, and it is true that people with integrity are honest, but they are also much, much more.

Many companies operate with a degree of integrity. We also know many that don't. According to Ernest Huge and Doug Park in 'The Best Companies Have the Most Integrity', great integrity in companies comes down to two things:[6]

1 **Being emotionally honest and open** – for example, not withholding information, such as why someone has been fired or promoted, the company's economic position or delaying bad news.

2 **Being principled** – behaving in a way that is consistent with stated values and beliefs and being uncompromising about principle.

Here are some examples of integrity in the workplace:

- Being sincere and not just telling people what you think they want to hear.
- Being real and genuine, not shallow and artificial.
- Being a 'promise keeper', 'walking your talk' and promising only what you will deliver.
- Being consistent and predictable.
- Being committed and reliable: saying 'I'll have the report done next Thursday' and keeping to that.
- Being candid and forthright, not political or manipulative or getting people to do things without them knowing your real intent.

It may be easier to count up the organisations that we know or have worked for that **don't** display integrity. It's important, when we think about integrity, to remember that it can only come from the individuals that make up the organisation. That is why, even if you are surrounded by a lack of integrity, if you want it, you need to start with yourself. Look at the list above and think about how often you yourself display these behaviours on a daily basis. There is a great saying from Alcoholics Anonymous about 'keeping your side of the street clean'. It means that even if someone is annoying you or behaving with a lack of integrity, all you need to worry about is yourself and your own responses. That means being responsible for yourself, your actions, and being honest about the way you yourself behave – even if people around you are demonstrating a lack of integrity themselves.

Integrity requires effort and conscientiousness.

Behavioural integrity, the alignment between words and actions, impacts trust and results. One study found that 'an improvement in only one-eighth of a point in the behavioural integrity score of

Stop and think!

Integrity is valued by employers as a much sought-after trait in employees. But employers also need to exemplify integrity at work. From high-level decision making to how people are treated, integrity will be reflected in a company's corporate culture. In a more interconnected and virtual world, it is likely to become an even more important quality as we collaborate across different cultures.

a hotel's managers led to a boost in hotel profits of as much as 2.4 per cent of revenues'. When it came down to it, this small movement was, in fact, down to the 'little things', as in keeping a promise, sticking to an arrangement made or following through on something.

Tony Simon, the Cornell associate professor involved in that study, says, 'Behavioural integrity is not about some higher **moral** code. It is simply about having words and actions that reflect each other.' If this is so, then isn't being late for something sending the wrong message completely? Isn't our inability to really focus, really listen to each other, actually saying that we really don't care? It gives the perception of a complete lack of respect for the other person, suggesting that they are less important to you. And perhaps they are.

Leadership experts Dr Gay Hendricks and Dr Kate Ludeman say that 'the mastery of integrity comes down to three things: being authentic with yourself, being authentic with others and doing the things you have said that you would do'. Maintaining authenticity is about self-awareness – knowing what you want out of life, who you are, what your positive characteristics are and your negative qualities and behaving consistently in line with your values. Self-awareness means you actually have to start thinking about these things in the first place. It's not something most of us naturally do!

Keeping commitments builds trust, and in a perfect world we would not break them. But it's become too easy to do just that, as we hide behind technology, our 'busyness' and our lifestyles.

Workplace integrity starts with honesty, decency and trust. It makes a difference to your professional development and in your immediate environment as it has an impact on others. You are not likely to be promoted if you are perceived as not being trustworthy or honest. Your day-to-day work is going to be pretty unbearable if your colleagues/employees/clients don't trust you or you don't treat other people well. And the higher your role in the organisation, the more important this becomes.

Integrity in the workplace can perhaps also be likened to that buzzword 'accountability'. Accountability means putting our word and reputation on the line. Someone is counting on us and we should care that someone is counting on us. But the realities of twenty-first-century business can make accountability seem daunting. Following through on a commitment used to be fairly clear and linear and followed a recognised framework or process.

Today's workplace commitments and projects can often be ambiguous, and we may need to create our own frameworks with many ways to reach a goal. In this context, being accountable can also mean being proactive and responsible. Responsible for outcomes, project results and, if you are in a leading role, also responsible for engaging employees and treating them well, as well as leading by example.

> if you want integrity in the workplace, always start with yourself

Developing integrity

Can integrity be developed? Of course it can, as it's your own personal choice. It can be developed in lots of ways, from deciding to be accountable and responsible to following through on your promises and commitments. Stephen Covey said: 'But until a person can say deeply and honestly, "I am what I am today because of the choices I made yesterday", that person cannot say, "I choose otherwise".' In other words, integrity is developed each and every day in the smallest of actions, as well as the bigger ones.

Integrity is about character. Can character be developed? Certainly it can! Being consistent, honest and doing what you say you will do, and practising this, is a great start. Have an opinion and stand up for something, don't sit on the fence. Think about what you value and the principles you hold dear and where these have come from. Some of these may be a product of your upbringing or conditioning and may not be traits or characteristics you want to keep. So knowing yourself is important. How can you be true to yourself and keep your side of the street clean if you don't know yourself, your strengths and weaknesses, what makes you tick and what you are accountable for? If you observe negative behaviour in others, you do not have to emulate it. That is always a choice.

In terms of your professional life, what sort of work do you do? Is this in line with your values and beliefs? If not, it's probably not the right environment for you. And in your personal life, what sort of relationship are you in and does it enhance your life and bring out the best in you, and vice versa? These, too, are connected with integrity because it will be easier to live a life of integrity if how you live and work is aligned to your inner compass.

Barriers to integrity

Some argue that integrity is closely connected with upbringing and early education and, of course, these do have a huge influence. Integrity, though, is an **internal** system of principles that guide our behaviour. Integrity is, therefore, a choice and, even though integrity is certainly influenced by upbringing and exposure, it can't be forced by outside circumstances. There are certainly factors that can encourage or discourage integrity. A person lacking in self-esteem, friendship and financial stability, for example, may be more likely to act without integrity. Someone else with higher self-esteem, a strong support system and a balanced life is more likely to act with integrity. Integrity comes from the daily practice of doing the right things.

Barriers to integrity are very likely to be linked to the human traits I mentioned earlier – greed, self-interest and pursuit of power – as these will influence what you do. For example, do I pay cash to my plumber so that he will give me a lower bill, knowing he is likely to pay less income tax on it or even declare it at all? Or do I justify it because I am not involved in some big tax scam and, anyway, everyone else is doing it? If I really want something, to what extremes am I prepared to go to get it? And if I want to display integrity, how difficult is that if everyone around me is not?

A life with integrity is an examined one. There will be times when we behave with what seems to be a lack of integrity or acting in our own self-interest. Sometimes that may be down to reacting to circumstances or lashing out because of pressure we might be under. Our ability to act with integrity may well be better demonstrated by our subsequent actions, such as learning what triggers stress responses and developing the self-awareness to look after ourselves, or by our ability to be honest, apologise and put something right.

If acting without integrity, such as deliberately stealing, lying or hurting others, is a choice, then what underlies that choice is how we justify the action. Today's choice for honesty seems to be 'it's OK as long as you don't get caught', or 'it's not that bad, everyone is doing it'.

Our speed of life and the urge to act in our own self-interest are definitely barriers to building integrity, as mentioned before. Things that become 'the norm', such as cancelling that meeting at the last minute, dictate the action. This can then escalate to bigger things as we find it easier to justify an action. We also seem to be so much busier than before, with numerous demands on our time, commitments to juggle and deadlines to keep. The more we juggle, the harder it becomes to keep promises.

'Whoever can be trusted with very little can also be trusted with very much' – this is a verse from the Bible. The message is that how you handle the small things will dictate how you handle the large. And we are certainly quick to judge others based on this. How many parents have told their daughters going on a first date that the way their date behaves at dinner, from addressing the waiter to simple table manners, will tell her everything she needs to know?

Barriers to integrity can also be created if one is easily influenced by current trends and norms and by what is going on around you. If you are working somewhere where it is 'normal' to fiddle expenses then maybe you will do it too if you're easily influenced, can justify your actions and make the active choice to do so. You are less likely to if you believe this is wrong and you choose to act by what you believe in. Perhaps we need more role models who can exemplify integrity.

10 steps to integrity

Here are ten ways to start developing your own integrity. It's always helpful to keep a record of what you are doing, or to at least record the processes you are going through and the results you experience.

1 **Start with working out what your values are**
   It can be helpful to start with your own values. These will be unique things that you value, that are important to you.

The first step is simply to write them down. The list could include anything, from 'being results-focused' to 'creativity' to 'patience' to 'respect'. Don't know where to start? Reflect and think about what makes you happy, what makes you angry, sad, gives you energy, tires you? And then think about the value behind that.

Examples: someone you work with is unfocused and distracted, often surfing the Internet or taking personal calls. This makes you angry because you are a team player and very results-orientated. Or your partner comes home from work early and surprises you by announcing he/she is taking you out for dinner. This annoys you because you value predictability, or it makes you happy because you love spontaneity.

Another way to discover your values is to identify your role models and write down why you like them – you will soon find common denominators in your descriptions that can indicate what you value. Or think about moments in life when you were on top of your game and felt unbeatable. What was going on at that moment – if you can identify those feelings you will find the values that match. You can do the same with times when you felt angry or frustrated.

Once you have a list, try to clarify these values – how are these values manifest (or not) in your life. Do you see them showing up in the work you do, the things you do day-to-day? If not, you can start to put this right. You can start making decisions that enable these values to be present in your everyday life. If competition is a value, for example, this can be fulfilled by the nature of your work and/or by playing a team sport. If love and caring are values, how is this visible in your relationships with your partner or family?

Every Sunday I sit down and plan my week. Not just what I am doing and when, but how each of my activities and actions are aligned to my values. For example, because having a strong work–life balance is extremely important to me, I plan my life around that value rather than allowing work and deadlines to eat into family time. At the same time, I still need to be accountable to work deadlines, but I also don't neglect to bake a chocolate cake! Both are important to me (and the chocolate cake to my husband and teenage stepsons).

2 **Be responsible**
It's easy to claim responsibility when things go well, but it's much harder when they don't. A truly responsible person, however, accepts responsibility either way. So next time you take on a project, be 100 per cent responsible for the outcome. Not a little. Not somewhat. Not pretty much. Own it 100 per cent – good or bad.

Start being more accountable. Keep promises and do things that you said you would do. Make commitments and stick to them. The more you do this the easier it will become, and it will also be enjoyable because all your relationships, both personal and professional, will benefit. Start with the little things and go from there. Ownership and accountability – demonstrate these.

We alone have the power to manage our lives and careers. The sooner we accept this fact, the better. Start being more proactive (see the chapter on being proactive).

3 **Listen more and multi-task less**
Consciously, actively and empathetically **listen**. Get rid of distractions. Lessen your technologically-driven multitasking and give other people focus and attention. You will be a far better communicator and you're less likely to cancel arrangements and fail to deliver. Be more thoughtful and respectful of others. Think twice before you pick up your smartphone to send a cancellation text.

4 **If you have to let someone down, do it with integrity**
If you absolutely do have to change an existing commitment, be open about it, state the problem, listen, get involvement

and solve the issue by agreeing a new commitment or an alternative solution. Can you do that with your smartphone? Probably not; unless you speak to the person or see them face to face it will be very difficult to demonstrate integrity and get the right message across.

5 **Manage your time well**

'No' is an empowering word. So every time you say or think the words, 'I can't say no', ask yourself if you can't – or if you're simply unwilling to. Take back your time in other ways, too: get rid of your to-do list (track projects and deadlines on a calendar instead); resist over-scheduling (you can't cram 12 hours of work into 8 hours, so stop trying); and estimate times realistically (let's face it, most tasks take longer than we think they will). Slow down a bit too. Plan your week, plan your day. Get up earlier.

6 **Tell the truth**

In the Jim Carrey movie *Liar Liar*, the lead character is constantly letting down his young son. On his birthday, his son makes a wish for his father to be unable to tell a lie for a whole day – this wish comes true. The character Jim Carrey plays is unable to lie, mislead or even withhold a true answer. For a day, why not see how much you tell the truth – white lies don't count, or do they?!

7 **Be personally accountable**

This, like responsibility, is a willingness to answer for the outcomes of your choices, actions and behaviours. When you're personally accountable, you stop assigning blame, 'should-ing' on other people and making excuses. Instead, you take the fall when your choices cause problems. Are you accountable for your actions even if nobody holds you accountable – or nobody catches you? You bet you are. So be your own 'accountability cop' and police yourself. On the long and winding road of life, choose accountability every time.

8 **Start with yourself**

If there is a problem or difficulty at home or at work, look first to yourself. Ask four specific questions: 'What is the problem?', 'What am I doing, or not doing, to contribute to the problem?', 'What will I do differently to help solve the problem?' and 'How will I be accountable for the result?'.

9 **Be boring**

Being consistent and predictable may sound boring, but in our world of uncertainty, rapid change and roller-coaster lifestyles, being consistent, reliable and predictable are positive attributes and they demonstrate integrity. Use them every chance you get.

10 **Manage expectations**

Of yourself and of others. The most direct route to self-empowerment is to be clear about expectations – not only what you expect, but also what's expected of you. To do that, you need to ask questions, make agreements and clarify. Otherwise, you risk suffering the source of much upset: missed expectations. Communicate clearly.

A day in the life of...

Let's take a magnifying glass to the skill of integrity through a day in the life of Sharon. We'll start with a brief introduction to Sharon, to give a quick snapshot of her life.

About Sharon

Sharon is in her late thirties, has two children at primary school and works part-time. Her partner works full-time. Sharon has a portfolio career, with several key clients for whom she delivers marketing and PR services. Sharon is quite stressed. Her life seems to be full of rushing around from one meeting or commitment to another; there is always something going on. Sharon is very good at her job but sometimes doesn't follow through on deadlines because of pressure piling up. Because she is good at what she does and has a positive disposition, she is often able to extend deadlines but she is aware of over-promising and under-delivering. She also often misses social arrangements with friends because of work pressures. Sharon juggles being a mum with all of this, but feels like she isn't doing that particularly well either. Recently she has started sub-contracting some of her work out to associates to help alleviate some of the pressure.

Let's have a closer look at a typical day in Sharon's life and how developing integrity can help her.

Sharon's typical day

Sharon gets up early and gets the children ready and takes them to school. She has a chat with the other mums at the school gate and then rushes off to the train station where she parks in the wrong place and gets a ticket. As a result, Sharon is late for her meeting so she checks her emails on her mobile while at the station. Sharon arrives at the meeting flustered, saying that the train was late. The meeting is about a new project and this time Sharon is leading a team of associates. They agree roles and responsibilities, though none of this is documented, and Sharon is confident that the project will go well. She ducks out of the meeting early, leaving the team to continue with their planning. On her way to pick up the children, she decides to cancel meeting with friends that evening as she doesn't feel up to it – she pleads a headache, which is sort of true. Sharon rushes home with the children and cooks. She eats their leftovers, as she forgot to have lunch, and heats up a take-away for her partner to have when he comes home. Sharon puts both kids in front of children's TV. She opens a bottle of *wine at 6pm and drinks half of it. It's been a tough day and she deserves it. Sharon thinks her partner really could be doing more to help with the household but it's never been discussed. She is too tired to talk to her partner when he comes home and, after putting the children to bed, Sharon stays up late watching TV and trying to wind down. She goes to bed quite late but does not sleep well.*

What's going on here?

Sharon's day is typical for many working mums in terms of what they have to juggle and be mindful of, but she is not handling any of it particularly well, even though some things such as cancelling her arrangements with friends and being late for her meeting could be easily justified. After all, who isn't rushing around these days?

However, as an ongoing lifestyle, quite a few relationships in her life are thinly stretched. Her work relationships are stretched because she is starting to become unreliable; the new associate relationships and project may unravel because expectations are not clear and because Sharon is not holding herself accountable. Her relationships with her friends (which could form a valuable support network) are suffering because she keeps cancelling at short notice. She isn't spending any quality time with her children. Her partner is last on the list so her primary relationship is suffering. And finally, Sharon is neglecting herself. So how can integrity help? It can help through raising self-awareness and creating more accountability. Sharon needs to clarify her own values first and what is important to her and look at her life through these. This will help her to be more in control and to make some changes. Integrity will also help with being more accountable and responsible and managing herself and her time in a different way.

What happens if Sharon starts putting some of the principles of integrity into practice?

Let's revisit Sharon's 'typical day' six months later.

How Sharon's life has moved forward

These days Sharon is much more at peace with herself and is starting to feel happier. She spent some time working out what was most important to her: her relationships with her family and having interesting, rewarding and fulfilling work as well as passion, security and fun. She could clearly see that none of her life currently was aligned to these values, and started thinking more about how she might be contributing to some of the pressures because of this misalignment.

Sharon decided to have a frank and clear discussion with her partner about their relationship and about how to share some of the childcare. Her partner was only too happy to give more support and, consequently, Sharon has two days a week when she does not have the responsibility of getting the children ready for school nor getting back in time to cook the evening meal. Sharon uses this time to plan her schedule and to catch up with emails. And sometimes she uses the time to go for a swim or to have a beauty treatment.

Sharon also calls a meeting with her associate team to look at how they can put systems and processes in place for team roles and responsibilities. She accepts that project accountability must rest with her and that, now she has a team in place, her own role is going to be much more about managing and leading that team. She actually finds she enjoys this type of role far more.

Sharon is also more aware of how cancelling or changing things, whether meetings with friends or extending project deadlines, is not really conducive to effective work nor strong relationships.

She really does value her network of friends and sees them as vital to her support and well-being. She knows that, these days, it's more acceptable to cancel things but she's making a more focused effort to only say yes to commitments when she honestly feels she can follow through.

And these days, of an evening, she more often than not finds time and energy to enjoy her children and spend evenings with her partner that enable her to relax and feel energised for the following day.

Sharon's example shows how integrity makes a difference day-to-day, and that this then has a positive ripple effect on fundamental relationships, decisions and life direction. Integrity is satisfying and rewarding because it means we can be our authentic selves and ultimately do and achieve more.

Interested in reading more?

Carter, S.L. (1996) *Integrity*. HarperCollins

Cloud, H. (2007) *Integrity: The Courage to Meet the Demands of Reality*. Collins Business

Covey, Dr S. (2004) *The Seven Habits of Highly Effective People*. Simon & Schuster Ltd

Fenstermacher, G.D. (2009) 'How Did We Get Here? The Loss of Integrity in American Life.' Speech at Pennsylvania State University
(You can download this speech at www.ebookbrowse.com or at www.the-advantage.info)

You can also find more tips, ideas and exercises by visiting www.the-advantage.info

'The pessimist sees the difficulty in every opportunity; an optimist sees the opportunity in every difficulty.'

Winston Churchill

Chapter 5

OPTIMISM

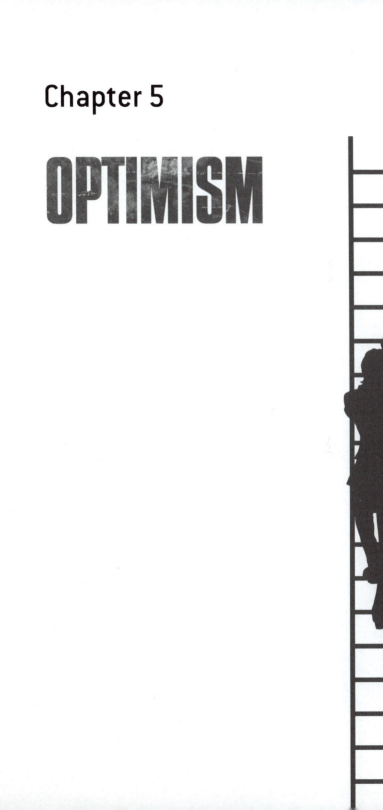

How optimistic are you really? How do you view difficult events in your life? Let's face it – there are a lot of things to feel negative about. And in an uncertain world where traditional supportive structures like secure employment and family are eroding, and we are experiencing challenges and opportunities like never before, cultivating and maintaining optimism is more important than ever. Research demonstrates that optimistic people are more successful, healthier and live longer. For many people there is an 'optimism bias' hard-wired into the brain, but for those who are more pessimistically orientated, the good news is that optimism can be learned.

What is optimism?

Optimism is often confused with 'positive thinking', as in viewing everything with rose-tinted glasses as a bit of a 'Pollyanna', no matter what the situation is. *Pollyanna* is a story that follows the exploits of a young girl, newly arrived in a small town, about the turn of the twentieth century. She holds the view that within every situation and each person is something good, and that this can be noted and amplified in such a manner as to make our existence easier, to make us glad that we are here. The Pollyanna attitude is used to describe someone who simply refuses to acknowledge any negativity whatsoever, and generally is used to refer to someone who is somewhat idealistic and outside reality in their thinking.

Our natural optimism bias can lead to irrational optimism, or what I call irritating optimism. For example, almost all of us believe ourselves in the top 20 per cent of the population when it comes to driving, having a successful relationship, or managing business. Almost all of us are irrationally optimistic about our health and lifespan – all of us like to think that we will live long and healthy lives. We also hugely underestimate the likelihood of losing our job or getting cancer. In business, optimism can lead to unrealistic forecasts. Those in sales know that over-optimism tends to produce over-commitment. Collective optimism can also lead to large-scale disasters. Over-optimism of a very large number of people about their repayment capacity on mortgages led to the housing bubble and recession in the United States. Irrationality and optimism are always at the very heart of any economic bubble. This can be referred to as 'systemic bias', which is the inherent tendency of a particular process to favour certain outcomes.

> overly optimistic assumptions can lead to disastrous consequences, but an optimistic bias can also inspire, motivate and protect us

Tali Sharot, in *The Optimism Bias*, says that we need to be able to imagine alternative realities and need to believe that we can achieve them.[1] Such faith helps motivate us to pursue our goals. Optimists generally work longer hours and tend to earn more. Economists at Duke University in the USA found that optimists even save more. And although they are not less likely to divorce, they are more likely to remarry.

Forget positive thinking

Positive thinking has a lot to answer for. There is a huge industry built on the back of positive thinking. Barbara Ehrenreich, in her book *Smile or Die: How Positive Thinking Fooled America and the World*, states that positive thinking has become a cult in the USA and that people are actually addicted to it. Putting on a happy face is the only way forward, no matter what the circumstances are. Any negative thoughts must be banished as they will, in turn, lead to negative results. Books such as *The Secret* by Rhonda Byrne, a huge bestseller worldwide, have not helped this trend and simply feed into an already vulnerable mind-set that accepts that everything that happens to you is dictated by the 'law of attraction'.[2] This then leads to irrational optimism where mind-set is all that matters. This can actually be very dangerous. *The Secret* sells itself by promising that 'Everything is possible. Nothing is impossible'. This sounds great, but the truth is we cannot change outcomes by thoughts and

> we can't reach our goals by thoughts and affirmations alone

affirmations alone. In fact, this statement is simply not true. We can achieve far more than what we believe may be possible by a combination of hard work, self-belief and healthy optimism. In that context anything, certainly, may be possible.

Psychology journalist Oliver Burkeman even goes so far as wanting us all to start thinking more negatively. He believes society's obsession with positivity is actually making most of us unhappier. In his groundbreaking book, *The Antidote,* Burkeman draws on personal experiences and scientific research to introduce a new, refreshing way of thinking called 'the negative path'.[3] The negative path is all about embracing those feelings we're taught to avoid – failure, pessimism, insecurity, uncertainty and anxiety. It's not about feeling gloomy, but instead seeing the bigger picture by being more realistic about happiness.

The realistic optimist

Some people say that they are neither an optimist nor a pessimist but a realist. But both pessimists and optimists can make realistic assessments of a situation. It is far more about how you respond to that situation that can define you as an optimist.

In a similar way that people have a preference for left- or right-handedness, based on the dominance of one brain hemisphere, neuroscience has discovered other opposing dominance characteristics between the left and right prefrontal cortex (PFC).[4] People who say that they are neither an optimist nor a pessimist but a realist may have a motivational system that reflects certain personality traits that lead to avoidance behaviours. These behaviours, through a combination of evolution and reinforced experiences, means they really are optimistic but just very cautious about that tiger hiding in the grass.[5]

The 'positive thinking movement', with its linear, over-simplistic solutions, ignores the balance that is needed between negative

glass half empty or half full? It depends!

and positive thinking and the different responses to adversity: action by approach (extrovert) or avoidance (introvert) personality types. An avoidant optimist's glass is neither half full nor half empty. It is simply at the level that he/she chooses to fill it to. Martin Seligman, a leading authority on optimism and positive psychology, says in his book *Flourish* that we've been living in a bit of a 'therapy century', and that the therapist's job traditionally has been to minimise negative emotion by psychological interventions that make people less anxious, angry or depressed.[6] Along the way, parents and teachers have joined in with minimising negative emotions. What is more essential, though, is to learn to function well even if you are sad, anxious or angry. The truth is that, even if you had all the therapy in the world, there will be days when you wake up feeling blue, worried or uncertain. What's far more important is to not only fight those feelings but to actually live your life heroically, which means functioning well even when you are sad. Abraham Lincoln and Winston Churchill were two severe depressives but also highly competent and well-functioning human beings who dealt with their 'black dog'. And the actor Stephen Fry openly admits to manic depression, which he somehow manages to rise above most of the time, and refers to himself as being an optimist. So perhaps he is one of the 'avoidant optimists'?

Genuine optimists stay grounded in the real world. They size up situations accurately and, if there is a problem, they face it and seek solutions. They play the hero in their own lives, which leads to personal growth and offers a real chance for improving any situation.

The hallmarks of optimism include:

1 Accurately assessing a situation, including asking questions, questioning assumptions, weighing up the facts, differentiating between facts and feelings and having a perspective.

2 Seeing problems as temporary and not pervasive. Being able to acknowledge your own role within a situation, feelings and actions. Less blame laid on self or external factors.

3 Having faith in your own ability to implement solutions, adjust and move forward constructively. Knowing that there is something you can do. You may not be able to change an external situation, but you can be more in control of yourself within it.

Why is optimism important?

Each of us really does have untapped potential and strengths that we generally do not use to the full. Our current economic and world situation invites us to step up to the plate and examine that potential, perhaps more so than we ever would have done otherwise. Another way of looking at the times we now live in is to view them as an exciting era of opportunity and change. Real optimism requires you to have your eyes wide open and not shut. Real optimism invites you to assess accurately the situation, face problems and take responsibility for your actions and seek solutions.

It's more important than ever, because optimism invites people to experience hopefulness and it also helps us to be more robust during difficult times. It enables us to be more accountable and proactive (see the chapter on being proactive).

While we can't say for certain why some people respond more positively to life's events, it's increasingly clear that your mental outlook can have a big effect on your physical health. Optimism motivates individuals to take control of their lives, while depression has been found to have the opposite effect. It is often linked to a sense of hopelessness because if you are depressed you can't engage in actions or events that will help to make your life better or solve a problem. The exact nature of the relationship between optimism and good health is still unclear. Martin Seligman says that it might be that optimists, as opposed to pessimists, are more likely to take care of their health because they believe in the potential positive outcomes. Or, it could be that optimistic people are more likeable and build better and more effective social networks, which have been associated with longevity. Another possibility is that optimistic people may have had less trauma or difficulty in their lives (a high number of negative events in a lifetime correlates with bad health). 'All of these are plausible', says Seligman.

Overwhelming evidence shows that an optimistic outlook, however that is demonstrated, provides a variety of emotional, social and health benefits. Some even argue that an optimistic outlook characterises normal rather than abnormal human functioning because it is so hard-wired into our survival.[7]

Positive people are also more likely to see opportunities, even when things are tough. This is probably more important than ever now. It is known that optimism is a necessary ingredient of resilience – the ability to thrive despite failure, set-backs and hardship (see also the chapter on resilience).[8] Optimism points towards being future-orientated and going back to that hard-wired belief that each of us does have, albeit to a greater or lesser extent, that things can indeed get better. Low optimism results in fear and uncertainty about the future, which in turn can result in passivity and not taking action to make anything better.

Optimism also relates to how we think about the past and, in particular, how we might think about the causes of

> things can only get better

anything negative. Optimists tend to believe that the *cause* of a negative event can be changed and that problems in one area of life won't necessarily lead to problems in all areas.

> In his book, *Optimism: The Biology of Hope*, Lionel Tiger argues cogently that optimism is not an optional characteristic in humans; it is as 'natural to man as his eyes that see, and as irreplaceable as hair'.

How can being optimistic help us at work?

Optimism in the workplace can help with the exploration of possibility, innovation and collaboration because optimism feeds into being more open to more opportunities. Generally, if you are perceived as being optimistic, you are more likely to get on well with your colleagues, be seen as a solutions-person and someone others want to be around.

Oprah Winfrey, when once asked what she wished she'd learned earlier in life, said 'I wish I'd known how to distinguish radiators from drains'. She explained that 'radiators' are people who give out warmth, honesty, positivity, energy and enthusiasm, which other people respond to. 'Drains' are people who are negative, downbeat, suck the energy out of others and don't like themselves. We can probably all think of people at work who we would consider 'drains'. At work, you want to be a radiator. That may not always be easy, especially if you work at the same place every day and are coping with pressures, set-backs, demands and challenges. But it's absolutely essential now. It's like cultivating your own immune system so you are better able to handle the pressures.

are you a radiator or a drain?

Healthy optimists are going to be good at evaluating a situation from different perspectives, weighing up different options and coming up with solutions. They'll be better at working within a team too.

An interesting survey of managerial roles at Hanover Insurance Group by psychologists Greenberg and Arakawa found that a manager's optimism didn't necessarily directly influence the engagement level of employees they managed but did have significant impact on their own engagement on the job, which in turn affected the performance of the team. Workplace engagement is currently a hot topic. It's been proven to lead to higher service and higher customer satisfaction as a result, because engaged employees use what's called 'discretionary effort' – they'll work over and beyond what is needed, leading to better business outcomes.[9]

Barriers to optimism

There are a number of barriers to developing positive optimism. Some of these are down to how we perceive what being optimistic actually is and some are down to our natural human tendency to irrational optimism.

Optimistic people are more likely to focus on the opportunities, but we also know that too high a level of optimism can cause potential problems to be ignored, leading to possible negative events or an over-optimistic estimation of a situation. It's like being overly confident. Lower levels of optimism are more likely to cause people to focus on the obstacles lying in their path, but if they are too pessimistic then they may never seize the opportunities in the first place.

Expectations and optimism

Some people believe that if we have low expectations then we won't be disappointed when things don't work out and will be pleasantly surprised if they do. As Homer Simpson says: 'Trying is the first step towards failure'. Actually, in practice there is sufficient research to show that having high expectations increases your happiness, regardless of whether you succeed or fail. What matters is how we interpret the events we encounter. Psychologists Marshall and Brown found that students with low expectations of their exam results were, yes, not surprised when they failed but they didn't **feel** better.[10] And if they did well, they put this down to 'luck'. Students who expected a high result and failed didn't feel worse because of failing. In fact, they felt inspired to do better the next time.

The positive illusion

Another possible barrier to healthy optimism is something referred to as 'positive illusion'. This is where individuals generally view themselves in a positive way, which is something that mentally healthy people do very well – perhaps too well sometimes.[11] The danger is when this personal view leads to biased behaviours to enhance personal quality of life.[12] It's easier to have an inflated sense of our own strengths but be less aware of weaknesses, or even of how we are perceived by others. Most studies find that people tend to have inflated views of themselves anyway. The research indicates that the relationship between people's self-evaluations and objective assessments is relatively weak. One explanation for this is that most people do have mild positive illusions (Taylor & Armor 1996[13]). This can influence decision making and an objective connection with reality. Perhaps this is why 'positive thinking' in the simplistic way it is put forward can actually be dangerous, as it can lead to an increase in 'positive illusion', which we all possess to a greater or lesser extent. It feeds directly into this and nurtures this.

The problem with affirmation and visualisation

One of the big problems with books like *The Secret* and the many other self-help books and articles on visualisation techniques and affirming that all is well, is that they give the wrong impression of a positive attitude and outlook on life and make it all sound so simple – that all you have to do is chant some affirmations and visualise yourself into a better place and so it will be. Hundreds of self-improvement techniques suggest that if you want a better job or relationship you simply visualise yourself into the perfect dream job or describe your romantic partner, and that by doing this you will start to attract the right kinds of decisions and influences into your life. People respond well to these sorts of messages because it all seems so easy. While a small element of this may be true (if you are positively expecting better outcomes, you may be more likely to put yourself into situations where these may occur), research and, I would argue, common sense put this on its head. In one experiment at New York University by Gabrielle Oettingen, individuals were asked to visualise their dream job.[14] Those who reported that they frequently fantasised about such success also reported receiving fewer job offers and actually often ended up with lower salaries. In another study, at the University of California, students were asked to spend a few minutes each day visualising themselves getting a higher examination result.[15] Even though they were only doing this for a short amount of time each day, it actually caused them to study less as a consequence and so get a worse result.

Could it be that many who focus on visualisations and affirmations are less equipped to manage the set-backs that may occur as well as putting in the hard work and effort needed to reach their goals? In order to visualise effectively you have to completely relax, and perhaps this too feeds into inertia. Perhaps many people are, basically, lazy and cannot or don't want to put in the hard work and effort needed for success. Short cuts and visualisation techniques are far more attractive.

The moody blues

It is true that optimism produces a positive 'mood', and this in turn is a big motivator for us. Our mood influences the way we view life and how we process information, and events will change depending on our mood, which in turn has an impact on our thoughts. Yet some people are very moody and 'up and down', with no consistency or predictability. How they respond to negative events (and even positive ones) is completely dependent on how they might be feeling at that particular point in time. We are all probably prone to 'moodiness' from time to time. Moodiness is related to lots of different elements, from genetics to hormonal influences, to natural disposition. However, significant progress can be made if an individual is able to come to accept that they have the power to control their lives and circumstances and their responses, rather than being swayed by every change they experience around them.

If your self-esteem is low, it may also influence how optimistic you are. Lower self-esteem can often mean that you automatically take responsibility every time you experience an event. For example, let's say you arrive at work (or school or a concert) and run into a colleague (or friend). This person doesn't acknowledge your greeting and actually looks away. One way of responding to this is to assume that you've done something to cause this: that you've upset this person, they're angry with you because of something you think you might have said the last time you met them.

This assumption can happen very, very fast and if you have low self-esteem you will be more prone to this. Healthy optimism says there may be a number of causal factors that have nothing to do with you: perhaps your friend/colleague has received bad news, wasn't wearing their glasses, was distracted or upset, in a rush, etc. Healthy optimists are less likely to automatically personalise events around them. However, even they are prone to assuming something worse if, on that particular day, they are experiencing stress or some upset.

If most of us show a natural optimistic bias (which can, as we now know, be irrational), how do we remain hopeful of keeping the benefits of optimism while at the same time still being aware of its possible downside? The answer is to be more aware of our own tendency towards optimism bias, have a better understanding of what being optimistic actually means. There is vast misinterpretation of optimism and being 'positive', and it's time we had a much clearer understanding of what I am going to call 'healthy optimism'. That means being self-aware, being in control of our responses, being accountable and being solution-orientated.

We need to think about how to build healthy optimism into our day-to-day lives, rather than a vague nod at 'being positive' or being in a 'good mood'.

Can optimism be developed?

A growing body of scientific evidence points to the conclusion that optimism may be hard-wired by evolution into the human brain. It shows that our brains are not just stamped by the past but are constantly being shaped by the future. A recent study scanned people's brains as they processed both positive and negative information about the future. The results showed that we are, indeed, hard-wired to be optimistic. Brain neurons will faithfully encode desirable information that enhances optimism but fails at incorporating unexpectedly undesirable information. So when we hear a success story, such as that of Mark Zuckerberg (one of the co-founders of Facebook), our brains immediately note the possibility that we too may become immensely rich. It's what keeps people playing the lottery too. But hearing something far more realistic, such as 50 per cent of all marriages fail, we immediately do not count ourselves within the half that might fail. Nor in the 75 per cent of second marriages that fail. Why? It comes back to our tendency to be

your brain is constantly being shaped by the future

optimistically biased. So we need to keep mindful of this bias, but at the same time, the fact that we have it means that healthy optimism can definitely be learned.

For example, why do some people write proposal after proposal to get their book published? They must know, on some level, that there is far greater probability of writing a book that few people will actually buy rather than a bestseller? They either have other reasons for writing the book or genuinely believe that theirs could be the bestseller. Or what about an actor who goes to audition after audition, despite the fact that a shockingly tiny percentage of actors actually earn a living from this career and an even tinier percentage become famous. They are likely to be passionate about what they do and see others achieve it, and so believe that success is a definite possibility.

Being mindful of this bias means we can still pursue our dreams but we may approach them differently or work harder and more proactively, setting clear goals and being in control. I probably submit around 30 work proposals a year, of which perhaps 2 are successful and result in a paid contract. Each time I submit a proposal I am convinced it will win and I know this is the right attitude to have. I also get better each time I write one. But I know that the end decision won't actually be about how good the proposal is. It will be decided as part of a short-list of equally competent consultants, using criteria based on a combination of cost, location and experience. Knowing this, I accept that I have to put in the work of writing 30 a year to get the 2, and I don't really worry about it too much or personalise the rejection when it comes.

Optimism and managing stress

There are two ways we typically approach a problem or stressful situation, whether that is a major life crisis or a day-to-day hassle such as being late because of a train being delayed. The first is emotion-focused coping, which is about trying to make yourself feel better by calming your feelings through meditation or relaxation or looking at the positives. The second is problem-solving coping, which means you are actively trying to turn the tide, decide what is needed and create a solution. It's probably better to use emotion-focused coping when it is too late to change the situation or when the stressor is outside of your control. It doesn't help, though, where you yourself need to take action to change an outcome. Wishing a huge project at work would get smaller or looking at the positives of producing it won't change anything, whereas tackling it and taking action will.

Faking it

Generally, we believe that how we feel influences how we behave. If we are feeling happy, we'll smile and if sad, we'll show a corresponding frown or grimace. However, even as far back as the nineteenth century, William James at Harvard University hypothesised that behaviour and feelings were a two-way street.[16] So, if you want to feel happy, start smiling. However, nothing came of this and for decades we have had self-help books telling us to change the way we are thinking and the behaviour will follow.[17]

The psychologist James Laird decided to test James' theory in the 1970s.[18] He got volunteers to create an angry expression by clenching their teeth and frowning and to create a happy one by smiling. The results showed that the volunteers felt much happier when smiling and much angrier when showing an angry expression. Subsequent research shows that this same effect applies to just about anything in our everyday lives. So, by acting, or 'faking it', you take significant steps towards feeling the way you want to feel. Behaviour first then feelings, rather than changing our thinking first. Much simpler!

Take confidence: most self-help encourages you to think about times when you've done well or were particularly proud of an achievement, or even to visualise yourself giving a confident presentation. But, if instead, next time you give a presentation you walk in with a confident stride, open body language and a smile on your face, you will automatically feel more confident. I've experienced this so many times that whenever I now give a presentation I prepare for it like an actor going on stage!

The ABCDE model and explanatory styles

Psychologist and author Martin Seligman says that the key to optimism and pessimism lies in our 'explanatory styles', how we explain life events (good or bad) to ourselves. The following model summarises this and, to some extent, we are all capable of responding in either way. Seligman believes that optimism can be **learned** and that anyone can learn it through asking themselves more questions before automatically defaulting into a negative response. Try it for yourself, and try to raise your awareness of how you would respond by default. Then keep asking questions to move towards healthy optimism.

Ways of experiencing an event	Healthy optimism	Negative response
Experience/negative event/problem/ situation or incident	More likely to look at event or experience positively. Will not see a negative outcome as 'negative'	Will scan for negative experiences and tend to find (or think they find) what they are looking for
Attribution and personalisation – the difference between personalising something and externalising it	Externalise – so you give yourself the benefit of the doubt. Don't automatically take responsibility for the situation or outcomes with no clear cause	Over-personalise – a tendency to solely blame yourself, even if there are very likely to be numerous other causal factors and reasons
Attribution pervasiveness – specific and temporary or global and permanent?	Tend not to blame yourself for an incident, i.e. getting upset and shouting doesn't mean I'm aggressive, forgetting my briefcase on the train doesn't mean I'm an idiot	Tendency to catastrophise by extending a specific situation to how you are all the time
Attribution permanence – temporary or permanent?	After deciding whether you have a role or responsibility in the negative outcome or situation, realising you have a weakness or problem to sort out and basically working on that problem. Or cut losses and benefit from self-perceived strengths	Continue to catastrophise and be resigned to the problem or issue being unsolvable

Ways of experiencing an event	Healthy optimism	Negative response
Dispute	Weigh all the possible explanations you can find. If you're at fault, you accept you did something wrong and put it right. Or you may decide the issue was not that important and either work on the things that are workable or preventable in future	Don't dispute anything. Instead, think of the first thing you can do to blame yourself and continue to focus on your shortcomings
Consequence/resolution	An optimist will accept that something unfortunate may have happened. You take ownership of your level of responsibility in it, resolve and plan to do things differently and move on	You're more likely to feel terrible about the consequences of the situation, give up and tell yourself there is nothing you can do

And based on this is Seligman's ABCDE model.[19] The model begins with the Ellis ABC model of Adversity, Belief and Consequence:

- **Adversity** (the event): My husband comes home and snaps at me.
- **Belief** (how I interpret that event): 'What a complete jerk. I can't believe he's being so disrespectful, aggressive and rude.'
- **Consequence** (feelings and reactions that result from that interpretation): I shout back, throw dinner away and leave the house angry.

In the journey to learning optimism, you have to first understand your own natural reaction to an event and your own interpretation and belief of that. Seligman usually asks his students to keep a journal for a couple of days to record various instances.

He then adds 'D' and 'E' to the model. These are Disputation and Energisation:

- **Disputation:** (provide counter-evidence to dispute either my interpretation of things or the cause of the event): 'I am overreacting. I don't like this shouting but maybe he's had bad news. It's not like him to be aggressive. He must have had a terrible day. Something has really upset him. I'm sure I snap too when I'm upset or angry.'

  This is certainly not an easy first thing to do in a situation. The natural tendency will be to react. Successful disputation, over time, leads to more positive feelings and a more realistic interpretation of events. It also means that we stop allowing an adverse event to dictate our response and that we have a better and healthier way of evaluating life experiences.

- **Energisation** is the successful dispute of negative beliefs and a happier outcome.

10 steps to optimism

Try out some of these approaches to raise your awareness and strengthen your healthy optimism. Try to record your experiences if you can. Even better, keep a diary, journal or blog for a few weeks.

1 **Embrace negativity**

  This doesn't mean being pessimistic but instead, as Oliver Burkeman says in his book *The Antidote,* accepting that negative experiences are just as important for our lives as positive ones. If you can accept that, then you'll be better equipped to develop a positive 'indifference' to negative thoughts or set-backs and have a better way of dealing with them. Life has its ups and downs and we need to embrace each and every one of them and grow from them.

2 **Rethink happiness**

Happiness can be yours right now – in fact, it is yours right now, not something that is forever in the future. Let go a little and relax. Go with the flow more. Take some time to define what happiness and wellbeing really mean to you – they should be about balance, rewarding work, a loving relationship, a network of friends and family, good health; many of these things are inside your control. So practise letting go of the things that aren't and accept them. That way lies real happiness and contentment.

3 **Act as if...**

Remember how powerful this is. Try adopting a 'power pose' for confidence – standing straight, shoulders back, chest forward, both feet grounded. If you're a habitual procrastinator, spend ten minutes acting as if you couldn't be more interested in what you're trying to do and start the task – you'll find that within a very short space of time you will have a strong desire to complete it. Or break things down into smaller steps first – the key is taking action, not waiting until you 'feel better'.

4 **Work out your explanatory style**

Monitor more how you respond to events in your everyday life. What is your default response if something does not go according to plan or you get some bad news? Take some time to understand yourself. After all, you're the only one who can!

5 **It's as easy as ABC... DE**

Try the ABCDE approach of dealing with a problem or any event. Record how you interpret something and what impact that has. What's important here is to realise that it's not the external problem or event that makes you feel a certain way, it is your own interpretation of it! Remember that Seligman's students practise ABCDE for a period of time and note down the results – and so change starts to happen.

Ditch the self-help books

For years I read self-help books. I was quite proud of my collection! For some reason they made me feel better, but I rarely carried out any of the exercises in them. Did you know that publishers of self-help books refer to the '18-month rule'?[20] They say that the person most likely to purchase any self-help book is someone who, within the past 18 months, bought a self-help book that evidently didn't solve their problems! They're making a lot of money and they certainly made a fair amount off me! So just get rid of books, affirmations and CDs, they will **not** make you happy or more optimistic. You have to do that yourself, and you CAN!

6 **Stop trying to think positively**

Apart from anything else it's exhausting and, if you become a Pollyanna by being continually overly positive, you may just find that you really start annoying other people. The way to healthy positivity is through getting to know yourself, taking responsibility and understanding how you tend to respond to things. After that, it's about taking action.

7 **Be a radiator**

If you can radiate energy around you, everyone will pick up on it. And if you're a drain, they'll pick up on that even more. Be aware of the high negative impact of being perceived as a drain. If you are having a bad day, try, before you enter the office, to centre yourself, ground yourself and take control. It takes effort but you don't have to let a temporary bad mood project on to everyone else around you. In fact, if you allow yourself to do that you'll only feel worse.

8 **Look for opportunities**

Become a seeker of solutions. There are always opportunities. Try finding them in any situation you have coming up – such as you were going to go on holiday but now can't afford it.

Opportunities for you include having a 'staycation' and getting to know your own hometown, spending time with family doing things at home or eating outside in your garden and acting as if you were on holiday. Or you have suffered a set-back at work. This is an opportunity for taking stock, reappraising your role at work and forging stronger communications with your team as you pull together.

9   **Find ways to relieve anxiety and worry**
We are all prone to worry and stress. It is up to us to manage ourselves to handle that. So look after yourself. If you're working hard to a deadline, make time for an early morning swim or treat yourself to a massage. Make sure you relax and switch off properly in the evenings so you can sleep well. The fact is that the more you can achieve healthy optimism, the less prone you will be to worry because you will simply feel far more in control of your life and are more likely to accept that events that cause worry and stress are a normal part of our lives.

A day in the life of...

Let's take a magnifying glass to the skill of optimism through a day in the life of Paul. We'll start with a brief introduction to Paul, to give a quick snapshot of his life.

About Paul

Paul is in his mid-thirties. He is single and lives in a house share in a large city. He is well qualified and has a Masters degree in Geography. After graduating he spent more than eight years teaching English as a foreign language in Japan, but returned to the UK when the language school he was working for went bust. For the last two years he has been working in administration for the City Corporation but was recently made redundant. He was kind of expecting it as there have been a lot of cut-backs lately and he wasn't getting on that well with his boss. He is quite heavily influenced by what he reads in the newspapers and hears on the news and feels generally pessimistic about the future. There are no jobs and, although he has updated his CV several times and applied for various jobs that fit his experience and background, he has not been able to find anything. He has a collection of self-help books on his shelf and, for a long time, was a great believer in using affirmations and positive thinking to help himself overcome his negative thinking tendency as he knows this is not healthy. Lately, though, these books are not really doing anything to help him so they are gathering dust.

He has a few friends, most of whom are in a similar situation. He feels depressed, although he has always felt slightly depressed throughout most of his life. Generally, he doesn't see much of a future for himself and dreams about going off travelling again and leaving the UK, as things just seem to be getting worse.

Let's have a closer look at a typical day in Paul's life and how building the skill of optimism can help him.

Paul's typical day

Paul usually gets up at about 10am and goes for a swim in the local pool or for a run. He has breakfast either at the sports club or at a café in town as he doesn't like eating alone in his flat. He goes to the local library and reads a paper and borrows a few books as he enjoys crime thrillers. He browses through some of the psychology section too. He goes back home and reads for a bit, surfs the Internet and looks at a few job recruitment sites. In the afternoon he has an appointment at his local unemployment office, where he has to legally attend on a regular basis. He gives them a bit of an update on his job search but doesn't get any real *encouragement or support. He tells himself, 'I really am a loser, not even the job centre can help me'. He buys a take-away and watches TV. Later that evening he meets with one of his friends, drinking a few cans of lager. They reminisce about the 'good old days'. The weekends are similar and Paul doesn't really do a lot of socialising, although he sometimes visits his sister for Sunday lunch. Generally, though, Paul is stuck and not doing much to improve or change his situation.*

What's happening here?

People with a pessimistic interpretation of events may naturally have a tendency towards doing so, as does Paul. Paul's main issue is how he is 'explaining' events in his life. At the moment he is doing this through the 'three Ps':

Personal – in that Paul feels he might be the cause of his redundancy. 'I was outspoken to my boss' or 'The boss didn't like me'. However, optimists would see the situation as not caused by themselves but by outside factors – 'My company was looking to cut costs and unfortunately my role was deemed superfluous'.

Permanent – Paul sees the set-back as permanent: 'I'll never get another job'.

The optimist would see the situation as temporary – 'This set-back is just temporary. Lots of people are being made redundant in the public sector but I can always go back to teaching English as a foreign language, either here or abroad, and maybe enhance my qualifications. I'll sign on first and get some unemployment benefit and then consider my options'.

Pervasive – Paul sees this event as pervading his whole life. 'I'm a loser', 'I'm hopeless' or 'I'm a loner'. He generalises one adverse event to all other areas of his life. An optimistic just sees one event, which may not even be adverse. 'This is actually great news! I hated the job anyway and this redundancy gives me impetus to look for a more fulfilling job. I've been relatively successful in getting work and I've had a very interesting life, having lived in Japan for eight years, and also I managed to save a lot of money there.'

However, Paul doesn't fall into this category as he is not naturally optimistic. He can start to try looking at the events in his life from different perspectives, though, and once he does this it will definitely help him. The difficulty is that the longer he allows himself to be in his current mind-set, the worse it may get. The circumstances themselves could become worse because of his current way of thinking about them. What this also means is that anything he reads in the news or any attempts to find work will feed into this mind-set, so he will be able to confirm that there are indeed 'no jobs' out there and that the situation is bleak. His friends, in similar situations, will confirm these views or, rather, Paul will attribute the comments he hears around him to supporting the whole negative outlook.

What would happen if Paul were to try and put some of the principles of healthy optimism into practice? Let's revisit Paul's 'typical day' six months later.

How Paul's life has moved forward

Paul is feeling better because he understands better his explanatory style and how he tends to interpret things around him. He recognises that he has got himself into a rather negative spiral and that the current external doom and gloom is only feeding into that. He has spent some time thinking through logically and understanding some of the world and national events that are part of the current economic situation and feels more accepting of them. He has started to realise that he can take some control over his own responses to things and experiments with looking at his situation from different angles. He actually has a lot of strings to his bow and is well qualified with international experience, so he spends a bit more time making sure this is explicit in his CV. He still goes for a swim in the mornings but has ditched going to the library and poring through newspapers. He catches up quickly with the news on his phone rather than spending time watching 24-hour news channels, as has been his tendency before. Paul has also been taking a few cookery classes and has made some new friends, and this has really had a great effect on him. He's looking after himself more and certainly saving money by cooking at home.

Instead of applying for jobs he has started to think more about what he has to offer and has been taking the initiative by visiting language schools and suggesting some opportunities for new types of classes that could be offered. He is actually quite confident, as he has been teaching and presenting for some years but lost touch with this skill after returning from Japan. He hasn't found a permanent job yet but he spends some time each day using a different approach to look for work, and he has started teaching a couple of evening classes on cross-cultural communication, using his experiences in Japan as examples. He's also started doing some volunteer work with disadvantaged young people in his local community. The volunteer work is adding some useful skills and experience but, more importantly, it makes a powerful difference in that Paul is starting to feel better about himself through helping others. He can see that he does have much to contribute and make a difference. He has also started to note down what he is thankful for in his life. Although gratitude journals are often a feature of self-help, they can actually be very valuable if used alongside positive optimism. For someone like Paul, who is prone to negativity, this is a useful and easy tool to gain perspective.

Optimism can be learned, it can be developed. It isn't something static that some people just 'have' and others don't, and positive thinking, by itself, will not help you to be more optimistic. We all need to start learning to develop healthy optimism. This requires becoming more self-aware and, to a certain degree, working on ourselves consistently. There are opportunities all around you to do this each and every day.

Want to read more?

Burkeman, O. (2013) *The Antidote: Happiness for People Who Can't Stand Positive Thinking.* Canongate Books Ltd

Ehrenreich, B. (2010) *Smile or Die: How Positive Thinking Fooled America and the World.* Granta Books

Seligman, M. (2011) *Flourish: A New Understanding of Happiness and Well-Being and How to Achieve Them.* Nicholas Brealey Publishing

Seligman, M. (2006) *Learned Optimism: How to Change Your Mind and Your Life.* Vintage Books USA

Sharot, T. (2012) *The Optimism Bias: Why We're Wired to Look on the Bright Side.* Robinson

Tiger, L. (1995) *Optimism: The Biology of Hope.* Kodansha America Inc.

You can also find more tips, ideas and exercises by visiting www.the-advantage.info

'If opportunity doesn't knock, build
a door.'

Milton Berle

Chapter 6

BEING PROACTIVE

Most people, if you were to ask them, would consider themselves to be pretty proactive. We have so much choice, information and freedom now, coupled with a strong sense of individuality, and we operate within that cosy bubble the majority of the time. We focus on results, making decisions, dealing with change and managing our complex lives. This sounds proactive but is likely to be far more reactive. Why? The fast pace of our lifestyles, the sheer overload of information and the increasing use of technology in every sphere means that we are living in more of a reactive way, perhaps even unintentionally. Living reactively, we feel we are getting more done as we multi-task our way through multiple demands on our time and focus.

What does being proactive mean?

The reality is that we are less effective, there is little time to reflect and we often don't realise that we are impeding our innate ability to be responsive. Being responsive means not immediately using our default reaction to every single comment and situation that comes our way. Being proactive means responding rather than reacting to stimulus. Whether we are responding or reacting, we can still come across to others as being energetic, highly motivated and active, which is why it's easy to think we are being proactive when we are not.

Each of us has the capacity to be proactive or reactive and there can be an underlying genetic bias in favour of either. Being proactive takes more brain energy as it requires us to make a choice and to actively think. Being reactive can be, and probably is, easier as it takes little thought to be so, and can even become a default behaviour without us realising it.

Stephen Covey famously said in his book *The 7 Habits of Highly Effective People*, that there is this small space between stimulus and response where we can choose how we want to respond to something.[1] So we literally have the power to control how we respond. Surely, now though, isn't that small space rapidly shrinking? Which means that, even if we are being proactive in some areas of our life, this may not be consistent or enough for it to make a real difference.

When you're proactive, you are creating situations based on a strategy you have created for yourself.[2] It's about taking purposeful action against a clear, specific goal. It's also about being more aware in the present. Proactive behaviour can be about changing yourself (personal development) or changing your environment through making suggestions, taking forward new initiatives and looking for opportunities to contribute in some way.

know the difference between reacting and responding

Reactions are triggered by circumstance; responses are tailored to it. It is, by far, easier to be reactive and our lives now positively encourage it because we are constantly rushing from one thing to another. So – how can we get back in touch with being truly proactive in our lives and tailoring our responses?

First of all, being proactive is a skill and a mind-set that we are all capable of. Anyone who consistently creates something of value is being proactive. In fact, often, our productivity in life is directly proportional to our level of proactivity. People who are proactive aren't just a little more productive than reactive people. Covey stated that people who take the initiative typically achieve, on average, **5000 per cent** or more quantifiable results in their lifetime. That's a massive difference.

So there are two aspects to being proactive:

- **Long-term and strategic** – this means being open for new opportunities, anticipating and preventing problems, persevering despite obstacles, achieving positive results and taking control of your own life. It also means being more self-aware and building in more of a work–life balance. You are using your own principles and values to make decisions.

- **Short-term** – this means small things you can do in the moment, how you use that space between stimulus and response and, more importantly, making sure that space gets bigger. Whether that is reflecting before you respond to that email, focusing and listening attentively, making time for yourself or taking a deep breath before you respond to an aggressive colleague or boss.

It boils down to these four things:

1 **Self-awareness:** this is the key to being proactive because if you're not aware of your negative reactions, it's impossible to take the initiative to change them into positive actions. You also need to know your strengths and weaknesses and why you are likely to respond a certain way.

2 **Willpower:** being self-aware does not, by itself, lead to proactive behaviour. In their book *Willpower: Rediscovering our Greatest Strength*, Roy Baumeister and John Tierney say that, together with intelligence, self-control turns out to be the best predictor of a successful life. However, we are not necessarily that good at exercising our willpower, so we need to practise that. *Willpower* is filled with advice about what to do with your willpower. Build up its strength, the authors suggest, with small but regular exercises, such as tidiness and good posture.

3 **Responsibility:** being proactive means having a sense of responsibility for your own life. That is 'response-ability', as in the ability to respond. Proactive people's behaviour is a

product of their own conscious choice, based on values and things that are important to them, rather than a product of their conditions, based on feeling.

4 **Self-mastery:** being proactive means having complete mastery over your thoughts, emotions and beliefs. It also means having control over your actions and never blaming someone else for your mistakes or negative circumstances. Being proactive starts with self-awareness and grows with willpower and taking responsibility for your actions. It is the key to creating personal happiness and the kind of life you desire.

When I think about my own life I can see these four elements clearly. I believe I have a high degree of self-awareness in terms of knowing and understanding my own strengths and weaknesses and why I am likely to tend to respond a certain way. Knowing this means I can always choose a different response, either in the moment or when it comes to planning ahead and taking specific action towards something. I may not always get it right, and exercising willpower certainly helps. Sometimes that can mean something very simple, such as being disciplined about my time or refraining from making a default negative comment, however much I may feel like doing so at the time!

I've mentioned earlier that I plan my week based on my values and what is important to me. This means I can be, and am, extremely productive both in my work and my leisure time. Perhaps, most importantly, I believe completely that I am in control of my actions (what I say and what I do) and in the choices I make about my life. I also take risks and make a lot of mistakes. If someone asks me to do something I have never done before, I am very likely to say 'yes'! If I am not happy with the way something is going, I am very likely to take steps to change it.

Why is being proactive important?

With so much uncertainty around us and circumstances that are definitely outside our control, many people struggle with anxiety, lack of sleep, worry and even depression as they face job loss, financial problems and other stress. Being proactive is a way of feeling more in control of our lives and of our futures. In a world that can seem out of control, proactivity is essential because proactive people don't allow the environment or their circumstances to dictate how they think and behave. They recognise matters over which they have no control and do not waste energy worrying about them. It's a choice, but it's a hard one for some people to accept. How many times do you hear people complaining or voicing their views on external factors, from the trains running late to the economic downturn? How many times do you find yourself reacting to stress or to feeling affected by the weather (especially when everyone around you is also complaining about it!)? How many times do you allow yourself to engage in idle gossip, which is another form of moaning? And beyond that, how many times do you take the initiative, whether it's to change something in your personal or professional life or to try something new?

Being proactive is important because only you can create the kind of life you really want, only you can be responsible for your reactions and responses to events around you and your circumstances, and only you can really be in control of your own happiness. You are far more likely to do that if you see yourself as the one at the centre of your life and the one in control of it. By focusing on what you can control – for example, your behaviour and how you respond and other factors that you can actually do something about – you start to expand your ability to influence others and influence your circumstances. But

> if you want to move ahead in your career or reach a personal goal or achievement, be proactive, resourceful and responsive

if you only zero in on what you can't control and allow yourself to be reactive or to blame others, this ability to influence massively decreases and you just get stuck in a negative spiral.

Being proactive makes you feel happier, too. By focusing on positive change, and by feeling more in control as a result, you are creating a situation much clearer from worry and anxiety. If you are stuck in anxiety and in focusing energy on preventing something bad from happening, you are likely to feel less happy and even less in control of anything.

How being proactive can help us at work

For a start, people's work has changed – we are far more likely to be moving jobs more often now, which means we have to be much more proactive and manage our own careers. If you engage in proactive behaviour you are more likely to be effective in your work and career and you are more likely to be working in the field that best engages your skills and talents.

Organisations themselves need to be more proactive and stay ahead of competitors. Smaller organisations tend to be better at this as they are able to respond faster. The flatter hierarchy can become in larger organisations, and the more autonomy managers can have to make key decisions, this will start to change.

People who are not able to be proactive in the workplace can easily become a liability. Why? Because it means they are more dependent on others and, therefore, require more 'maintenance'. In today's workplace it's no longer about just getting the job done. You now

don't be a liability

need to be a self-starter and focused on how you can make a difference. Work has grown far more complex, so now proactive behaviour could also be seen as the differentiator for keeping your job. Be non-proactive at your peril.

Criteria for proactive behaviour at work include doing something that is self-initiated, change-orientated and future-orientated. Here are some examples:

- An intern asks for feedback on her performance (self-initiated) so she can work out what skills to develop (change-orientated) and can add a testimonial to her CV or LinkedIn profile (future-orientated).

- Someone in a junior position does something unexpected but incredibly useful and valuable, without being asked: a personal assistant provides her company director with a folder of useful conferences and events that are worth attending for networking purposes (self-initiated) in the coming year (change- and future-orientated).

- A project manager approaches his appraisal by conducting a self-evaluation of recent projects (self-initiated), coming up with examples of how he can stretch his skills (change-orientated) for new projects (future-orientated).

Being proactive at work can also be viewed as having foresight and acting ahead of anticipated events. So, the more efficient you can be in managing day-to-day tasks effectively, the more nimble and open you are going to be, which encourages proactivity. If you're proactive you are far more likely to plan, set yourself goals and manage your time well. If you are proactive you cause things to happen rather than waiting to respond after they have happened. You are active rather than passive.

A review on proactivity at work (Grant & Ashford 2008)[3] emphasised that today's workplace of flat hierarchies and dynamic conditions, which has only become more so since this review was done, demands a different kind of employee. What is needed now is an employee who is future-orientated and a self-starter not needing constant supervision and instruction. Grant and Ashford also argue that, 'Employees do not just let life happen to them.

Rather, they try to affect, shape, curtail, expand, and temper what happens in their lives.'

How proactive you might be at work is, to some extent, influenced by personal and situational factors. If you feel, as an employee, that you have a lot of autonomy and freedom to make work decisions, then you are more likely to be proactive because you feel more confident to do so. According to a 2010 review by Bindl and Parker, there is ample evidence that this proactive behaviour at work is strongly influenced by the atmosphere in an organisation, its corporate culture and its management.[4] So someone who may naturally be proactive may be less so at work if the environment is not conducive. If you're a company wanting proactive employees, then create the kind of atmosphere to allow that to flourish.

The benefits of managers who encourage proactivity are huge. Proactive employees tend to show increased work performance, more entrepreneurial success, higher commitment to the organisation and higher job satisfaction. And the organisation flourishes through, in itself, being proactive and competitive.

Another recent study (Gerhardt, Aschenbaum, Newman 2009) showed that when employees are allowed to set their own goals and manage their own time and environment, they perform more productively.[5] The study also recognised that proactive skills can be taught to those who may not naturally have them and recommended that employees who demonstrated these skills already should be actively encouraged to use them to the fullest benefit of the whole organisation.

Networking is definitely seen as a proactive behaviour. Networking is not the transactional 'working a room' approach, but about building genuine relationships, both face to face and online through social media channels. LinkedIn is now the number one recruitment site because companies recruiting can search easily for specific skill sets.[6] A good LinkedIn profile is now seen as being more reliable than a CV – this is because it is quite difficult to lie on your LinkedIn profile; if you've been to a particular university, for example, you are likely to have connections and endorsements that reflect this. LinkedIn makes it easier to show off your projects and work, and recommendations from others who know your work. Best of all, LinkedIn allows you to connect with as many people as you wish and create many different professional connections.

> relationships are the key to successful networking on sites such as LinkedIn

Whether networking on- or offline, it's still about nurturing relationships, visibility and transparency. So, just as you can't expect to walk into a crowded room and make meaningful connections without looking to help or collaborate with others, sticking a profile up on LinkedIn and not actively following the professional network etiquette is not being proactive. And what is the etiquette? Aside from the obvious things regarding how your profile is written and a clear headshot (the equivalent of being appropriately dressed for a business function), you need to be interacting with your network by posting interesting articles, inviting others to connect with you using more than the generic LinkedIn invite message, seeking out and offering opportunities. All of this is self-initiated, change-orientated and future-orientated.

Barriers to being proactive

Woody Allen once famously said that '90 per cent of life is just showing up'. To some extent this is true, I suppose, but proactivity has to be more than merely 'showing up'. If we are proactive by nature, we are also more likely to be resilient and positive (see the chapters on resilience and optimism), and we need to be because we are likely to take a lot of knocks. If you're being proactive, you also have to be prepared for rejection and 'no' answers. If we are not proactive by nature and take a few knocks and are not resilient enough to bounce back, that might prevent us from being proactive in the future – i.e., 'I did show up but nothing happened!'. Proactive people persevere in their efforts. They won't be happy with saying things like, 'Well, at least I tried' or 'I did my best'.

Proactive personality traits have been proven to be related to other personality dimensions, such as extraversion and openness to experience.[7] So if a person is naturally introverted, this may prevent them from being as proactive as they need to be. However, the available research also clearly shows that proactive behaviour comes from more than just personality. It's also strongly driven by situational cues, such as an autonomous environment or a supportive coach, for example. So someone who is introverted can be influenced to be proactive positively by a coach and can be coached towards changing their behaviour and reaching desired goals, thus becoming the driving force in their own life.

> being an extrovert doesn't necessarily mean you'll be proactive, and being an introvert doesn't necessarily mean you won't be

Being proactive can make demands on your time and mental and physical resources because it often means doing things over and beyond what might be expected or required. Some people are naturally lazy or don't want to be bothered with making an effort to be proactive. Again, this is a personal choice. 'Effort is one of the things that gives meaning to life. Effort means you care about something, that something is important to you and you are willing to work for it.'[8] (Carol Dweck, *Self-Theories: Their Role in Motivation, Personality, and Development.*) It could well be that people who 'don't want to be bothered' really do mean it, and if there is something that they care enough about, they are actually able to find it in themselves to be very proactive.

Another barrier to being proactive is a tendency to blame circumstances for a negative situation. This will then result in reactive behaviour. So, if someone treats you badly and you respond by reacting aggressively or negatively, you are more likely to feel bad as a result. If you are proactively pursuing a goal, suffer a set-back and then blame your circumstances, you are defaulting to being reactive. Therefore, being proactive is strongly connected with optimism (see the chapter on optimism) because optimistic people will tend to think differently about set-backs or a negative situation.

Our fast-moving lifestyles also mean that, in the short term, that space between stimulus and response is very small. We are busy and focused and flit quickly from one deadline and task to another with energy and flair. We consider ourselves to be proactive when actually it's just more of the reactive. So our very perception of what being proactive means can be, in itself, a barrier.

> that space between stimulus and response is getting smaller and smaller

Procrastination can be a huge barrier to proactivity. According to Dr Piers Steel, author of *The Procrastination Equation*, 95 per cent of us are procrastinators![9] And some of this must surely be driven by our frenzied lifestyles and shorter attention spans. We surf the Internet instead of tackling that project, or we put off making an important phone call or a crucial task because something else today has eaten into our time. We all do this to a certain extent so that means we are all prone to procrastination and this can threaten our ability to be proactive. So planning and self-discipline have to be key components of being proactive.

Probably one of the biggest deterrents to being proactive is fear. This is usually fear of the outcome, i.e. rejection, failure or just something changing. That is why doing things in small steps that help remove that fear is important. Find ways to remove that fear and you will take more risks, be more innovative, feel more confident and be more proactive. And that is a virtuous cycle, as the more proactive you are, the more risks you are likely to take because you feel more confident and in control.

Can we develop proactivity?

I revisit Stephen Covey here because proactivity is such a central focus of his book *The 7 Habits of Highly Effective People* and the very first habit is being proactive and responsible for our own lives. Viktor Frankl (Holocaust survivor)[10] says there are three central values in life: the experiential (that which happens to us), the creative (that which we bring into existence) and the attitudinal (our response to difficult circumstances). What matters most is how we respond to what we experience in life. Proactivity is grounded in facing reality but also understanding we have the power to choose a positive response to our circumstances. It's also about understanding what factors we can influence and what we can't. There is no point in devoting energy to things outside of our control, but by focusing on elements we can ourselves change, our chance of influencing those very things we can't control seems to magically change!

If being proactive is a habit, then habits can be learned. It is said that it takes 21 days to form a new habit. However, we know from things such as resolutions made at the beginning of a new year, that many of us cannot even last 21 days. It's as if we've forgotten how to stick at things. Think about the Olympics. Olympian athletes spend years perfecting and honing something very specific in order to compete. They believe in their abilities, their resilience in the face of adversity and in the opportunity to triumph. And

think like an Olympian

they keep at it. Their mind-sets, their attitude, their determination, rigour and their psychological processes are applicable to anyone seeking to be proactive. The clearer your goals and the more excited you are about them, the more motivated you will be to achieve them. Habits are developed when we believe they are worth developing.

So, if you want to be proactive then the goals you set for yourself need to be things you really want to do. And you need to make time for planning and setting them. Not many people sit down and plan their lives, their years, their months, their days. Sure, some of us make to-do lists, keep diaries and so on, but it's not the same. There is a long-term aspect to being proactive, as we know, and that is where the goal-setting and life management comes in.

How we respond in the moment and day-to-day is the short-term aspect of being proactive.

Remember:

- **Long-term and strategic** – this means being open for new opportunities, anticipating and preventing problems, persevering despite obstacles, achieving positive results and taking control of your own life. It also means being more self-aware and building in more of a work–life balance. You are using your own principles and values to make decisions.

- **Short-term** – this means small things you can do in the moment, in that space between stimulus and response. These things may include reflecting before you respond to that email, focusing and listening attentively, making time for yourself or taking a deep breath before you respond to an aggressive colleague or boss.

> to be proactive in the short term means being more thoughtful and reflective, as well as more self-aware

In order to be proactive in the long term, it's important to develop foresight. This means learning to anticipate problems, understanding how things work and looking for patterns while at the same time not expecting how things went in the past to be a predictor for how they might go in the future. Proactive people are able to pre-empt possible obstacles by working out ways to manage them in advance.

The role of education

Education and training can definitely help develop proactivity, and research supports this.[11] Parents can help children and teenagers to be proactive, and indeed must if they are to develop strong proactive habits later in life. When a child meets with failure or problems, it's important to help him/her understand how to interpret that and what actions can be taken to improve the situation. It's important for a child to learn that he/she can impact his immediate environment for the better by actions taken, and that even if those initiatives don't work out, he/she can try something else.

> It is a great aim to help a child set goals and then work to achieve those goals. However, if we don't do this ourselves, it might be hard to teach this to our kids! Anything that enables incremental progress, such as learning a sport or a musical instrument, encourages proactivity.

Young people need to be taught to be proactive because of their natural tendency to react to situations based on their feelings at the time. Obstacles become overwhelming to anyone when too much time is spent on them. This saps energy and creates hopelessness. Teenagers need to learn how to focus on specific personal goals, create a plan of action, outline necessary steps and set a deadline. Parents and carers need to demonstrate a problem-solving way of thinking. If young people have a role model, whether that's a parent, teacher or other respected adult, and they see this person solving problems without complaining or worrying, they will want to imitate this productive and proactive mind-set. Help your kids take responsibility for their lives but do the same yourself! That means not being a victim of circumstances, not being reactive yourself, nor blaming others.

I mentioned the role of coaching in developing proactivity and this can be very beneficial in goal-setting and being accountable to someone else for carrying out the action needed to achieve those goals. Quite often people are not proactive because they just have low levels of accountability, both to themselves as well as to others.

Teaching proactivity is made up of two main components:

1 taking responsibility for action instead of expecting someone else to think for me, and

2 systemic view – an ability to understand how making a change or shift now will impact something in the future.

Both of these can be taught, but they also need to be practised often and in a positive way. Taking responsibility for action (being accountable) has to do with several emotional skills, so this can be harder to teach. For example, a fear of failure that leads to avoidance has to be treated differently than resistance to change.

10 steps to being proactive

Try some of these to help you develop your proactivity skills, both in the short and long term. The results you experience may surprise you! Try to record your experiences and what happens as a result.

1 **Watch your language**
   For a full day, or for as long as you can, heighten your awareness and listen to your own language and the language of people around you. How often do you hear reactive phrases such as 'There's nothing I can do', 'I have to do xxx' or 'That's just the way I am'. Try re-scripting these to more proactive language, such as 'I have lots of different options',

'I choose to xxx', or 'I can use a different approach and see what happens'.

2 **Commit to being proactive**
Think of something you have coming up where you might normally behave reactively, or where you might normally not consider taking the initiative. This might be something at work or it may be a personal situation. What might be a proactive way to respond? Remember the gap between stimulus and response and make a commitment to choosing your response.

3 **Light up the room**
For one day try to be a light, not a judge; a model, not a critic. Choose to be part of the solution, not the problem. Try this in your relationship, in your family, in your work. Try it the next time you are in a meeting or having a conversation. Don't engage in moaning, gossip or blaming. Work on the one thing you have control over – you!

4 **Eat the elephant one bite at a time**
If you find yourself procrastinating, putting something off or just not giving something your full focus and attention, break things down into manageable steps and celebrate incremental progress. What's important is to take that first step. Writing a report? Can you get the headings and the structure done? Set some manageable goals for yourself, achieve them and track your progress.

5 **Slow down**
If you're constantly rushing from task to task, deadline to deadline and day to day, it's easy to feel out of control rather than in control. Take time to reflect. Take time to plan your week, take time to plan your day. And that doesn't mean a checklist of things you have to get done. It means conscientiously thinking about how you want to approach different situations and events and what goals you want to pursue.

6 **Take stock**

Think about what is happening at the moment at work or home. Are things how you want them to be? What are some things where you can initiate changes? If you're not working and want to, what changes can you make to your skills and experience to help you find fulfilling, interesting and rewarding work? Do different things or do things differently if something isn't working. If you wait for it to change by itself, it won't happen! Scan for opportunities as much as you can. And when those opportunities come, grab 'em!

7 **Learn something new**

If there is something you've always wanted to try, now is the time! Want to learn to sing? Go for it. Travel to an exotic place? Volunteer in a disadvantaged community? Learn to bake? We have so much capacity in us for learning. If you particularly go for learning something you previously thought you would not be able to do, taking steps to reach that goal will significantly develop your ability to be proactive. I love baking but there was a time when I was hopeless at it and didn't even enjoy it. I taught myself to bake and I did this quite deliberately. It helps me focus on detail and precision, which I don't find natural since I prefer to look at the big picture. What is funny, though, is that others perceive me as being a great baker and being good at it, when actually I find it quite difficult!

8 **Start something in your community**

When I first moved to the town where I now live, I dreamed of starting a community gospel choir. I decided to do it and, despite initial rejection and personal misgivings as to whether I could do it or not, I moved forward with it and we now have a strong, powerful choir with 80+ members, from which I get extraordinary satisfaction and fulfilment. It's hard work and not always easy but nothing can beat what you get from knowing you've started something yourself.

Look for opportunities to start something. And if there is something you have always wanted to do or be part of in your community – if it does not exist already, make it happen!

9 **Don't talk about the weather**
In the UK we have this compulsion to talk, moan, rave and go on and on about the weather! It's easy to engage in this banter and it's even easier to react to it when someone throws weather comments your way. See if you can stop talking about the weather just for one day. It may seem like a silly thing to do, but when you think about how strongly weather seems to affect our daily actions, you can see that it is one more thing we are giving energy and focus to that is outside our control. Be proactive, enjoy whatever weather the day brings and choose your response when someone else moans about it.

10 **Whatever it is, begin it**
Goethe said that 'boldness has magic and genius' in it, referring to following a goal or dream by taking the first step towards it. Take action. Don't stop at the idea stage. You may have to first define what that goal is, but once you have, start. You are the only one who can!

A day in the life of...

Let's take a magnifying glass to the skill of being proactive through a day in the life of Mark. We'll start with a brief introduction to Mark, to give a quick snapshot of his life.

About Mark

Mark is an undergraduate studying media and arts. He isn't sure what he wants to do when he graduates and hasn't really thought about it much. He enjoys his media studies and considers himself lucky to be studying something that is a genuine and strong interest of his. He's good at his studies and works hard, getting good grades (he's headed for a First) and is a great communicator, whether that's giving presentations, managing a team project or preparing a report. Mark has an active social life and takes full advantage of everything student life has to offer. He has a steady girlfriend, a great relationship with his family and generally life is good. He's done a little bit of work experience but not very much. The long summer break is looming ahead and, as yet, Mark has nothing planned. He might work part-time at the local supermarket and use the money to travel. He knows the job market is tough but he is a confident young man, very likeable and gets great feedback on all his work and team projects. He thinks he will have no problems finding well-paid work on graduation, although he hasn't put much work into updating his CV. Mark lives in a house share. His parents have already told him that when he graduates he is welcome to move back home and that there is no rush to move out given the tough economic climate.

Let's have a closer look at a typical day in Mark's life and how building the skill of being proactive can help him.

Mark's typical day

Mark is just finishing his second year of studies. He gets up fairly late as he has no lectures today. He meets up with his girlfriend for coffee and they chat about what they are going to do this weekend. Mark goes to the library at lunch to finish an essay he needs to hand in. He thinks about doing some work on his dissertation topic for next year but decides to put it off – it's such a long time off and he's sure he'll come up with a good topic over the summer. In the afternoon Mark takes part in a student debate on the cost of studying. He thinks himself lucky as he started his degree before tuition fees increased. He's not really affected by the increases but thinks he should support the cause anyway. He then attends a seminar and contributes actively to the discussion related to a lecture earlier that week. Later that day he ambles off to the student bar to meet up with some friends and talk about summer plans. The afternoon stretches into the evening, when he goes for a bite to eat with a group of friends, plays a round of pool in the student bar and enjoys a few more drinks.

What's going on here?

Mark sounds like a lovely young man and he probably is, but he is in real trouble here. He is so relaxed and positive that he is not really anticipating change ahead and thinks he is well equipped to handle the upcoming challenge of finding work when he's anything but. The reality is, though, that jobs in the media industry are extremely hard to come by without any experience and, even if a few years ago Mark could have got by on his charm and high grades, it's not going to be enough in today's tough climate. Although Mark is not a reactive person, as such, he still gives the perception of being quite lazy and he's not really taking any responsibility for his life and its direction. He's coasting a bit, and for a while this will work because of his personality and likeability. He is also obviously intelligent, hardworking and has some good skills that he could be making more of.

His parents are not really helping by reassuring Mark that he can move back home. They are, in their own way, feeding into a self-fulfilling prophecy of a tough job market for graduates and, therefore, no jobs. They see all their friends' children moving back home so mean well, but just because it's tough out there doesn't necessarily mean there aren't any jobs going.

One day, Mark goes to a talk held at his university about the soft skills you need to get ahead. He's curious as he thinks he has quite strong soft skills.

What happens when Mark starts to put some of the ideas about being proactive into practice?

Let's revisit Mark's 'typical day' six months later.

How Mark's life has moved forward

Mark is now in his final year of studies. He decided not to travel over the summer after all and, instead, spent half the time working and saving a bit of money, as he reckons this might be useful for when he graduates, even if he does not have large debts to pay off. He definitely does not want to move back in with his parents when he graduates so he is quite motivated. He also managed to get some work experience with a reputable media company – it was only for two weeks, unpaid and very basic, but he has focused on the transferable skills it has given him and he is making more of these and working on how to best describe his soft skills in his CV. He also went into the work experience with a bright attitude, determined to learn and exceed expectations, even when he didn't feel like it.

Today he is up early working on his dissertation. Although the company he did work experience for did not want to offer any promise of future work, Mark asked them if there was a particular project they wanted support with and he is making this part of his dissertation. Having a focus like this helps him have more excitement about the dissertation. It's a huge project but he's broken it down into more manageable chunks and has started planning his week more effectively to do the work, rather than waiting till the last minute. He plans to present the results and his findings to the company next spring. Mark hopes the company may offer him more permanent work as a result, but even if they don't, his dissertation subject is so topical he feels more confident about using this as a tool to help find work. As it's Mark's final year he is looking for other opportunities to get work experience and to do this alongside his studies at weekends and in the evenings. He has a couple of interesting leads and is following these up. Mark presents well so he always tries, wherever possible, to get a face-to-face meeting. He has learned that just sending out an email isn't going to get anywhere. Mark is also planning ahead for when he graduates. He's managed to get an extension on the house share so will be able to stay there, for an affordable rent, for a further six months after graduating.

That evening Mark goes out for dinner with his girlfriend. She encourages him to set up a debate himself to help other students be more proactive. For Mark this was not easy to do at first, but now thinking more about what he wants to do and planning is starting to become second nature.

Here we see how proactivity is crucial, even to someone who is actually doing quite well, because these days that is not enough. We really need to up our proactivity to get ahead and to lead more rewarding lives. It is the only way to move forward.

Want to read more?

Baumeister, R. and Tierney, J. (2012) *Willpower: Rediscovering Our Greatest Strength*. Allen Lane

Covey, S. (2004) *The 7 Habits of Highly Effective People*: Personal Workbook. Simon & Schuster

Steel, P. (2011) *The Procrastination Equation: How to Stop Putting Things Off and Start Getting More Done*. Pearson Education

You can also find more tips, ideas and exercises by visiting www.the-advantage.info

'Success is going from failure to failure
without losing enthusiasm.'

Winston Churchill

Chapter 7

When the world is stacked against you, do you rise or do you fall? Do you lash out or do you survive? We all know people who've overcome some amazing obstacles. We may even think, 'Would I be that strong?' if faced with a similar situation. On the flip side, we all know people who've completely gone to pieces when life throws them a curve ball: people who just lose it and can't seem to get it together, no matter what.

What does resilience mean?

Resilience is the ability to respond well to pressure, deal with setbacks effectively, respond well to change and challenges and, basically, bounce back. Most importantly, it is not a fixed character trait but an ability and a capacity, which means it can be developed.

Resilient people are goal-orientated, which gives them a reason to get back up and keep going in the face of adversity. They don't give up easily, if ever. Resilient people know their own strengths and they know that they can depend on themselves to do what it takes to get the job done, even if this means going it alone. Yet they can also call on

> resilient people get right back up when life deals a set-back

support if they recognise they need it. They keep a sense of proportion, knowing what is reasonable and what is impossible.

Resiliency is actually built into the human brain as what's known as an 'adaptive survival mechanism'. This is a behaviour, strategy or technique enabling us to survive. This means that some of us are naturally very resilient and will be able to cope well, even with early stressful life events. However, it also means that some of us may not be as resilient, either because we are not naturally as resilient (down to genetics) and/or due to lack of supporting factors in our environment. This is best explained as follows:

How resilient someone is comes down to three main areas:

1 **Personality/individual characteristics:** Resilience is seen as an innate ability that forms part of your personality. This is why we perceive some people as just being far better able to handle set-backs than others. Personality traits here include: the extent a person feels in control of their lives, perseverance, emotional awareness, optimism, perspective, sense of humour, self-belief and the ability to problem solve.[1]

2 **Environment:** Resilience is wholly dependent on your experiences and how you interact with your environment. So, factors external to you will determine how resilient you are, such as how much social or family support there is in place at the time.[2]

3 **Person and environment:** Resilience is a product of a person's personality, in combination with external influences such as family, peers and social environment.[3] What this means is a combination of 1 and 2. Someone with both a personality prone to resilience as well as strong environmental support may well be incredibly well equipped to deal with set-backs and difficulties as they go through their lives.

It is also true that we build resilience simply by going through adversity. We all know of people who have suffered enormous hardship while growing up, and yet emerge from this as powerful human beings making a great success of their lives. We also see the opposite. This is where the personality and environment issues mentioned come into play. The extent to which they are there is what determines just how resilient someone may be.

I believe I probably am naturally resilient, but also that I have built up my resilience by experiencing difficult times growing up. Part of that included having very broken schooling, which meant I had to gain my education as a mature student in my twenties as a single parent. But not having ever studied mathematics properly and a fear of numbers meant that it was extremely difficult for me to get into the leading business school of my choice to do an MBA in my thirties. I failed on the first two attempts because of my lack of numeracy skills and was told in a personal phone call from the subject Head of Finance that I should apply somewhere else. Most people probably would have accepted that but I believed I could somehow learn those basic maths skills that would enable me to pass the numeracy test. I'd done brilliantly in all the other assessments and the interview. I requested one last go to get in, even though this was not normal policy. This was granted and I spent two weeks with an A-level maths tutor learning all the mathematics skills I should have learned aged 18. I passed the test, got into Cranfield and ended up taking Finance electives in my second year and doing very well. And the Head of Finance later admitted he had been wrong about me!

I believe resilience is something that we **can** learn and develop (and need to), even though some of us may be more naturally disposed to being resilient than others. This is not to say, though, that we need deliberately to seek out adversity in order to build better resilience!

However, adversity can develop resilience. A recent study, which focused on studying people's resilience in connection with the economic recession, showed that capacity to be resilient **increased most** during the toughest of times and was not worn down by all the uncertainty and rapid change.[4] This proves, then, that we do have far more capacity to cope than we think.

Resilient people tend to view life's difficulties, regardless of how many there are of them, as challenges and respond with action.

What I mean by this is that they are almost accepting of the fact that there will be set-backs and challenges in life or in a specific endeavour but feel in control enough to respond, rather than be reactive. Set-backs force us to take risks, learn and grow. And we probably live in a time where there are unlimited opportunities for us to develop our capacity for resilience. In fact, you may be far more resilient than you think. Because everyone has experienced set-backs – it is part of life.

> accept set-backs, embrace them, look for the opportunity in them

Optimism is also an important element of being resilient – choosing to focus on maximising strengths and accomplishments and choosing to look at the positives in a situation. The ability to do this and to learn from adversity is dependent on how you interpret set-backs or problems triggered by personal choice or by choices of others. There are two classic ways of responding to adversity, both of which have a connection with optimism and positive psychology (see also the chapter on optimism). The first is to assess a situation critically and the second is to take it personally. An example of this is, let's say you did badly on a piece of work or a project that you worked very hard on. Your response to this can be to tell yourself: 'I have been under a lot of pressure lately and haven't been sleeping well. Even though I worked hard, I know my mind wasn't really focused and I wasn't able to give this my best shot' – critically assessed. The second way of dealing with this set-back is to say to yourself: 'I did badly because I am just not good at this. I'm obviously not the right person for this kind of project'. Positive psychology suggests that the healthier way of viewing adversity is the first one. The more you personalise a set-back, the harder it is to bounce back from it because the second method suggests something more permanent that you cannot easily change: 'I am just no good at this kind of work', which, of course, may or may not be true.

Think about this like exercising – the more you consciously practise this the stronger the skill becomes. Speaking of exercising, this is correlated with strong levels of resilience, maybe due to the endorphins produced and feeling physically stronger, or both. If we believe there is a connection between body and mind, then exercising and being fit and strong physically and building that strength may also help increase resilience skills. So going to the gym may be even better for us than we think.

Why is resilience important?

In these dynamic conditions, you're going to fall on your face a lot. You'll need to bounce back in record time, learn from your experience and attack the next challenge with equal boldness. If you are not able to do this successfully, there is a real danger that each time you fall, it will take longer to get up.

On the one hand it's the external conditions around us that mean we need to be resilient. If we have just lost our job, we can't afford to not bounce back quickly. But resilience is also important simply because the dynamic conditions mean that we need to be willing to try new things and venture into places we have not been, or maybe where no one has been before. It's far easier (and comfortable) to do things the way they have always been done but that is not going to work now. Taking risks and trying new things inevitably means we will make mistakes, and that is where resilience comes in.

I think being resilient can also buffer you against what may feel like risky behaviour. To thrive in the current environment I believe one probably has to take more risks than ever. My husband, for example, has recently changed his work voluntarily, purposefully to pre-empt a work situation that he felt could otherwise, in the next few years, change dramatically and not in his favour. So, although things were going really quite well in his current employment, he felt that the nature and corporate culture of his firm would not help him to develop the long-term value needed. So, instead, he has joined forces with a trusted colleague to help set up and run a boutique consultancy firm – more risk but also potentially more reward, both emotionally and potentially monetarily, and certainly better in terms of work–life balance. It also gives the opportunity to present the very best of himself, up his game and sharpen his skills. It's exciting, and potentially the best career move he could have made. It's going well and he seems much happier with this decision, even though there are also huge challenges ahead of him. So, being resilient is also being more aware of opportunities and actively seeking those out, **ahead** of any potential adversity or problems. Resilience is, therefore, also about taking control.

As well as increasing individual resilience, it will become more important actively to seek out formal and informal support networks, both face-to-face and virtual, to buffer against the changing dynamics of the workplace and society in general. We see this happening more and more with sites such as LinkedIn, and other social media that have become the 'after-work economy' of informal drinks and dinners, where relationships, networking and your personal credibility really matter.[5] Resilient individuals tend to have strong social networks.

A 2010 survey of senior executives by Accenture supports the importance of resilience. Of those surveyed, 71 per cent said that resilience played a key role in whom they decided to retain. And 77 per cent associated resilience with seniority, saying that senior leaders were either 'very' or 'extremely' resilient compared with 36 per cent associating resilience with those at middle management or below. However, the most interesting point about this is that they concluded from this research that 'resilience may be the new criterion for professional advancement and that in the current economic uncertainty and fierce competitiveness, organisations that prepare their upcoming leaders to be resilient will have a distinct advantage'.[6] But it's not just leaders who need resilience – most jobs have huge pressures and the potential for set-backs and disappointments to occur.

Barriers to developing resilience

Why is it difficult for some people to persevere? It's because perseverance is about sustaining effort and interest. These days we lose interest far more quickly than ever before because we have so many options available to us in the first place and because we have cultivated a society (particularly in the West) of immediate gratification. If attention is a hot commodity, we are quite capable of getting excited about multiple projects and achieving none.

And those who believe in fixed intelligence or mind-set will also find effort hard to embrace. What this means is that some people believe that if you have what it takes to be talented or gifted by nature, then not much effort should be needed. A growth mind-set, though, believes in embracing challenges and seeking out new learning opportunities and developing a grittier perspective. Malcolm Gladwell's book *Outliers* shows strong evidence that hard work and practice is necessary for anyone to be truly successful, whether they are a sportsman/woman, inventor, businessperson

> 'success is 99 per cent perspiration and 1 per cent inspiration'
> Thomas Edison

or musician. The raw talent may well be there, but it's the hard work and effort that leads to success.

Developing resilience takes effort and determination. These may not be qualities that come naturally to everyone. If one is naturally risk-averse, for example, then developing resilience will be harder.

Yet, we can build our capacity to be resilient. Contrary to the idea of some of us just being stronger than others, resilience can be built around what support and connection we have in our day-to-day lives.

Developing resilience

Just how do you do that? How do you stay upbeat in the face of rejection or disappointment, or just day-to-day pressures that seem to be increasing for all of us? Resilience is an amazing thing, but if you don't have it, how can you get it?

Know how to deal with C.R.A.P.

TED conferences bring together talented and successful people from across the globe from the fields of technology, entertainment and design to give 10- to 15-minute presentations on a topic.[7] Richard St John gives a great TED talk about success and he mentions eight key points, one of which is the acronym C.R.A.P.[8] You have to be able to deal with C.R.A.P. to be truly successful. The acronym stands for the following, and I think they sum up resilience really well:

- **Criticism** – if you are going to take risks, grab opportunities, make changes in your life or indeed for any type of new initiative you take on, you will face criticism. You have to be able to handle and deal with criticism.

- **Rejection** – we know this is going to happen more than once in life. If you can't bounce back fast, you will have problems.

- **Assholes** – everywhere in life we are going to encounter people who are aggressive, drain our energy, want to take credit, or want to exert power and influence over us; it's unavoidable and you have to be able to deal with them!

- **Pressure** – we are under more pressure than ever before and there will always be pressures and deadlines. We have to be able to manage ourselves effectively to handle these pressures with grace and ease. Otherwise they will handle us.

The best way to handle C.R.A.P. is accepting that you will face these elements and have strategies in place to deal with them. It's almost like a boxer in the ring – if you're rejected, how

know how to deal with C.R.A.P.

long will you be on the ground for? If you're dealing with someone who is aggressive, what are better ways of responding to this that don't ruin your day or zap your own positive energy? How can you plan and manage your time to handle the pressures?

Equipping ourselves to respond to adversity

Why is one person able to bounce back more easily than another? Take two different people who have lost their jobs. Let's call them Jack and Kyle. Both of them respond by being sad, listless, anxious about the future and indecisive. Jack gets his head together after a few weeks of this, tells himself the economy is going through a bad patch and that he has marketable skills. He updates his CV, sends it out to dozens of companies in his network and gets rejected by them all. He then tries six more companies, using a more thoughtful and focused approach and eventually lands a position. The position may well be in a different field and applying his skills in a different way.

Kyle, on the other hand, spirals into hopelessness, believing he got fired because he can't perform under pressure, and does not try again because of a paralysing fear of failure. He begins drinking in the evenings because he feels depressed.

It comes back to the classic ways in which we tend to respond to adversity based on that combination of natural characteristics and personality traits, together with the type of support network we have (or have had in the past) around us. In Jack's case, he may naturally be more resilient and have the strong support of family and friends. Kyle, on the other hand, may be less resilient naturally and may not have strong family support. He may possibly also have other issues going on in his life that means he is more vulnerable to pressure.

Resilience can be developed, and in fact does develop, without intervention through life experiences. We don't necessarily have to go through repeated experiences of adversity. For example, people who are made redundant more than once become inoculated to the psychosocial effects second- or third-time round. They find ways to cope.

Learn optimism

Martin Seligman says, in his book *Flourish*, that the key to building resistance is learned optimism. His research shows that people who don't give up and are resilient have a habit of interpreting set-backs as temporary and changeable, and suggests that people can be taught how to think like optimists.

The Penn Resiliency Program, designed by Jane Gillham, PhD and Karen Reivich, PhD, has introduced an innovative set of lessons for young people.[9] Based on cognitive-behavioural theory, the Program teaches resilience skills by introducing resilience concepts through role-play, short stories and cartoons.[10] These are then practised using a variety of tools for solving problems and difficult situations, which are based on real-life situations. The skills practised are assertiveness, negotiation, decision making, social problem solving and relaxation. These projects are now being taught to teachers in Australia and the UK to train them in how to deliver resilience skills. The same type of training has also been developed and is being successfully used in the US Army. Although these projects are in their infancy, let's hope that such training does begin to become more mainstream.

Gain self-awareness

There are also stress inoculation training programmes, known as SIT.[11] Essentially, this is a cognitive-behavioural treatment that is used to help a person gain confidence in their ability to cope with stress and anxiety related to a trauma of some kind. The way it works is that a therapist helps a client become more aware of what triggers stress and helps them come up with coping strategies, which are often simple things such as relaxation and deep breathing. This is resilience training of a kind, as these methods develop self-awareness. Self-awareness is the cornerstone of making any kind of behavioural change – it means you know your strengths and weaknesses and you understand underlying patterns of why you do things a certain way. It also means you understand what can make you stressed, angry or irritated and can start to develop strategies and responses that are more effective than lashing out at others or becoming debilitated by stress.

Develop grit

There is considerable evidence that educational interventions in young people can increase their resilience. 'Grit', in psychology, is a person's perseverance and passion for long-term goals and their innate ability to overcome obstacles to reach them (Duckworth *et al* 2006).[12] Gritty people are simply more likely to overcome adversity and push themselves towards success. However, again, this is an ability that has been lost somewhat by our desire for things to be far more immediate, which in turn is compounded by our modern lifestyles and by technology. This means that if things don't happen quickly for us, it's easier to justify giving up.

how much grit do you have?

Martin Seligman suggests that the more education a person has, the more grit they have, but which comes first? Does more education produce more grit or, more likely, do gritty people persevere through many failures and set-backs and go on to get more education? An experiment conducted by Seligman also showed that older people have more grit than any other age group, with the over 65s having far more, which probably correlates with having gone through more different types of experiences and natural set-backs, enabling resilience to be built.

10 steps to resilience

You can develop your ability to be more resilient – try these ten ways to build buffers and become stronger emotionally, psychologically and physically.

1 **Getting perspective**
   Life is always going to have challenges, set-backs and some adversity. One of my favourite quotes is from James Taylor's song 'Shower the People', in which he sings, 'into each life some rain must fall'. Ultimately, we CAN choose the way we think, feel and act in response to circumstances. It may feel very hard to do that sometimes, but we each have the capacity to do this. And, quite simply, the more you do this the better you will become at it. Keep asking questions: 'How can I learn from this experience?', 'What is the most important thing in this situation?' and 'What are some other ways I can choose to look at this?'. The better the questions we ask, the better answers there will be. Use questions to get the right perspective to tackle the situation. Make the effort and find time to do this. Be thoughtful about what you do and the decisions you make.

2 **Don't wallow in the mud**
   Think about what happens in a really bad thunderstorm. If you only look at the mud on the ground, you can't see the blue sky above you. The mud is your past. Leave it behind and don't stay stuck in it. Personal set-backs can prevent

you from seeing your true potential and being able to see those new opportunities I talked about earlier. But we CAN shape and influence what is yet to happen. Think about what matters to you now. Ask more questions like 'What's the next step for my best interest and happiness?' or 'How can I make a difference in this situation?'. Keep making choices and moving forward. Take control over your life – you're the only one who can!

3 **Ask for help**

This is about creating that supportive network around you. Resilient, successful people take responsibility for finding the right support to solve a problem or to help themselves. It's like having your own personal board of advisors – people who can help give a fresh perspective or a certain expertise, or just listen to you and be there for you. Surround yourself with people whose character and opinions you respect and trust. Join clubs and social networks that are close to your interests and values.

4 **Know your strengths – trust and use them**

It's important to know what you are good at and where you excel. So many people can get stuck in work that is absolutely not right for them. This economy now demands that we step up and work to our strengths so that we can be the best we can be in our work. If you are not sure what you're good at, then find out! Try new things. Use diagnostic tools that can help understand your personality and character traits. The best person to get to know is always yourself!

5 **Keep your options open**

There are more possibilities and opportunities than we can possibly think if we only keep ourselves open enough to them. Start by knowing what success and happiness really mean to you. If something isn't working, look for other ways of approaching the situation. If you are trying to set up something new, keep trying things in different ways when you experience a set-back or obstacle. Adopt an attitude of never giving up.

6 **Build proactivity into your life**
If you're proactive, then you're going to pre-empt adversity by your actions – i.e., asking for help when you need it or making some changes in your work, like my husband did. Practise interpreting events in an upbeat way and focusing on positive action that you can take to improve or change the situation, whatever it is.

7 **Look after yourself**
This means taking responsibility for your mental and physical health. Get enough sleep, build in balance, exercise regularly, have a massage or acupuncture so that you are physically resilient and alert – there is a strong connection between body and mind. Eat nutritionally balanced meals. Think about practising meditation and Yoga too. General Casey, former commander of multinational forces in Iraq and former Delta Force hero, said: 'The key to psychological fitness is resilience'. Physical fitness is the other half of psychological fitness.

8 **Focus on what you can change and accept what you can't**
Stephen Covey called this your 'locus of control'. This means not wasting time and energy on factors outside your control and knowing what things you can control and what you can't. You can control your responses to any situation, so focus on choosing your response wisely instead of reacting. Change your response and attitude; respond well and you build resilience and confidence.

9 **Celebrate failure**
You are always going to miss 100 per cent of the opportunities you don't take. So you may as well take them. Develop an attitude of actually celebrating failure. Why? Failure can be your launch pad for change. Failure is the very best way to learn absolutely anything, and build stronger

self-awareness. Take on the lessons learned from failure and do it differently next time.

10 **Take more risks**

Yes, that's right, more risks! In a world that's changing as fast as ours is, the riskiest thing you can do is be stable and take no risks at all. Remember that making mistakes builds your resistance. Ever heard of the movie *The Yes Man*? In it, Jim Carrey plays the role of a guy playing it safe and ends up lonely, bored and without a job or relationship. He decides to say 'yes' to everything that comes his way, with life-changing consequences. Practise saying 'yes' to opportunities and challenges. Just for one day. And then perhaps a little more. You can learn to take risks, and doing so builds confidence. Start with 'low-stake' risks, such as trying a new route to work or saying 'yes' to an invite to coffee, and build from there. Try to plan risk into each day and week and build it up.

A day in the life of...

Let's take a magnifying glass to the skill of resilience through a day in the life of Malcolm. We'll start with a brief introduction to Malcolm, to give a quick snapshot of his life.

About Malcolm

Malcolm is in his late fifties. He's close to the official retirement age but he knows he will probably, very likely, have to keep working because his pension is not going to be enough to live on. He's a financial analyst for a large company and his job has been becoming more and more demanding in recent years. Projects have been short term with less repeat business. The company has made some cuts and bonuses have become very inconsistent. Luckily, Malcolm made quite a bit in the boom years and has managed to save. In the good old days he had a personal assistant too, but that stopped a while back. As did any business-class travel on overseas trips.

Malcolm is generally quite easy-going, though he does have a natural tendency to worry and wants to please. He's always focused on working so, although he has a small social circle, these tend to be other couples he and his wife have known for some years.

He's married and his wife is successful in her own right. The children are grown up but their youngest son, who graduated recently, has moved back home as he can't find work. Malcolm and his wife also have three young grandchildren, whom they see regularly. They live in a large, bustling city.

Let's have a closer look at a typical day in Malcolm's life and how building the skill of resilience can help him.

Malcolm's typical day

Malcolm gets up at 7am and heads for work on public transport. He tends not to have breakfast as he is in a rush and doesn't normally feel that hungry in the mornings. He grabs a cappuccino at the station café. The rush hour is, as always, very bad, and today he manages to spill coffee on his trousers, which really irritates him.

Malcolm arrives at work, where he's working on an exciting project with a new team who are all quite young. They are very on top of social media and networking and they see this as a key way to start to win new business and projects. They are always coming up with new ideas and are full of energy. Malcolm doesn't really understand social media and thinks he is just not the sort of person who would find it easy to use. Most of the time he ignores it because he just doesn't have the time and he typically has far too many emails to respond to anyway.

The morning tends to zoom by in a flurry of meetings and dealing with correspondence and, before you know it, it's time for lunch. Malcolm pops out for a sandwich at lunchtime but doesn't really take a break as there's so much to do. He comes back from lunch but tends to feel quite demotivated by this time of the day, the reason for which he can't put his finger on. Consequently, his afternoon is not very productive and when he runs into his boss at the water cooler, he doesn't feel on top of any new projects and believes he came across poorly, although actually his boss was in a terrible rush and didn't have time to talk to him.

Malcolm decides to work late that evening to try and make up for wasting time in the afternoon. He manages to get through his inbox and notes that the new team are setting up a discussion forum on the company's intranet to put together a social media strategy. He idly wonders if he should attend but quickly decides this is something best left to the younger generation.

Malcolm gets home quite late and eats a reheated dinner his wife has cooked. They have a quick glass of wine and a catch-up before watching some news and going to bed.

What's going on here?

Now, on the face of it, Malcolm's life seems fairly run-of-the-mill. Things are ticking over OK, he has a job and nothing too awful has happened. Is he even in need of any resilience skills? Of course he is, and he knows at the back of his mind he has a need. There is a danger, though, that Malcolm will get left behind in terms of his work and that he is not protecting himself sufficiently from adversity nor building the resilience skills he will need if, for example, he were to lose his job. His company has been making cutbacks but it is also in debt and is not planning on paying out any bonuses in the medium- to long-term future. He hasn't been pulling in any lucrative projects and isn't on top of things at all regarding social media. He's clearly under pressure but doesn't seem to be handling it that well. He's also not looking after himself – he doesn't eat meals regularly and those he eats are not necessarily freshly prepared. He doesn't appear to do much exercise either. It's easy to not take a lunch break and to work late in the evenings, telling yourself that you're being productive, but the question is are you really being effective at this time? It's also a common side of pressure to take things personally, such as when he encountered his boss at the water cooler. But part of that was also connected with Malcolm's own awareness that he isn't being very productive and he probably knows he isn't bringing in enough meaningful projects to the company.

He dismisses the idea of getting to grips with social media by attending the discussion forum, when this might be the very thing to help him get started. And the fact is that, even though he stayed late, it probably didn't make that much difference to what he achieved.

What would happen if Malcolm developed his resilience skills?

Let's revisit Malcolm's 'typical day' six months later.

How Malcolm's life has moved forward

Malcolm is healthier these days and looking after himself more. He's started walking part of his way to work and makes sure he eats a little breakfast in the mornings, even if it's only a banana or muesli bar. He also gets to miss some of that rush hour and takes the bus instead. Because his company has actually been embracing flexible work, two days a week he now spends an hour at home catching up with emails before leaving for work, and so misses the rush hour completely on those days. He finds this makes him more productive. He decided to be more proactive at work and now has regular check-ins with his boss to discuss new projects, having put together a clearer strategy for himself. He did this by taking some time to take stock of his life and where he wanted to be with this work. Malcolm eventually stopped putting if off and decided to dip his toe into social media, and this was a good thing, given that the company generally is now starting to become far more active on Twitter. What Malcolm has discovered, to his delight, is that Twitter has proved to be a really useful tool for understanding more about his industry and the marketplace and, although he doesn't post regularly, he is certainly looking at it more and is starting to contribute some articles related to his area of expertise. Social media generally has also given him an unexpected bonus of a stronger communication channel with his children. He's also keeping an eye out for other work opportunities, and both he and his son are working on improving their LinkedIn profiles. Through this he has started to keep in touch with other colleagues who are now working elsewhere.

When Malcolm was asking himself those questions he also thought about his strengths generally. He realised that he had perhaps, to some extent, pigeonholed himself at work and, although he is not ready to make any drastic changes, he is becoming far more aware of where he can contribute most and this is giving him confidence in what projects to put forward. He also remembered that he used to be quite good at computer games and loved playing them with his kids when they were younger. This makes the step into social media less daunting and something that he may start to also get quite good at. He has also rediscovered his love of music – this was something that he shared with his wife and they used to go to many concerts together. So, now they have started to go to concerts again after work, which gives them both a lot of pleasure and much-needed relaxation time.

Malcolm still tends to worry. But he is calmer these days and feels more in control. He's more likely now, for example, to understand that something like the water cooler incident is down to how he himself is responding, and the stronger and more secure he feels the less likely he is to take this sort of encounter personally. He is more likely to cope better with ongoing pressures and, in the longer term, is equipping himself with stronger resilience skills.

You need resilience skills to cope in the times we now live in. If you're not naturally resilient (and even if you are), you now know there are simple things you can do to become more resilient day to day that help you not only deal with set-backs and rapid change, but also help you to pre-empt potential difficulties and challenges.

Interested in reading more?

Clarke, J. and Nicholson, J. (2010) *Resilience: Bounce Back from Whatever Life Throws at You.* Crimson Publishing

Gladwell, M. (2009) *Outliers: The Story of Success.* Penguin Books

Reivich, K. and Shatté, A. (2002) *The Resilience Factor: 7 Keys to Finding Your Inner Strength and Overcoming Life's Hurdles.* Three Rivers Press

Seligman, M. (2012) *Flourish: A Visionary New Understanding of Happiness and Well-being.* Simon & Schuster

Seligman, M. (2006) *Learned Optimism: How to Change Your Mind and Your Life.* Vintage Books USA

Zolli, A. and Healy, A.M. (2012) *Resilience: Why Things Bounce Back.* Business Plus

You can also find more tips, ideas and exercises by visiting www.the-advantage.info

THE
BEGINNING

You've reached the end of this text but it's actually only the beginning – the beginning of your own journey into tapping into these inner resources that we all have.

What I wanted to do in *The Advantage* is to explain why a determined focus on key personal skills is vital in today's world. The skills that give you 'The Advantage' are more about developing your individual competences and skills, and they will give you so much more than the 'traditional' team-building or leadership skills. By working on developing these skills, you will be so much more effective in your own role and when you are in a situation where you might be leading people, you will have the resources you need to do so. If you suffer disappointments, you will be better equipped to handle them. If you are anxious or worried, you will become so much stronger and able to cope. And you will be more productive, happier and relaxed, with strong healthy relationships, and live a life filled with meaning and purpose.

It is about application and work. I continue to work on these skills each and every day; probably even more so as a result of writing this text. Much of what I write about in *The Advantage* seems so obvious, but if it is, then why are so many of us either not even aware of these things or not as good as we could be at these skills?

Everything I have written about begins with self-awareness. It is the cornerstone of emotional intelligence and starts with understanding who we are, why we think the way that we do and how we tend to respond to change, difficulties and opportunities too.

It's about taking the time to really think about what you say and why; what you do and why you do it. And then think about what you will say or do before acting. It's about really knowing our strengths and weaknesses and harnessing and managing these to be truly effective and to fulfil our potential.

We are all fearful of change and of putting ourselves in new situations, to varying degrees, but it's so important now to recognise that we have to embrace change or be left behind. And the only way to embrace change is to start with small steps, repeat them and build on them each and every day. Start now!

The seven skills outlined in *The Advantage* naturally overlap. In the 'A day in the life of' sections at the end of each chapter, I magnify one particular skill but actually we need to develop all seven and apply them holistically, not just to specific situations and circumstances but to our whole life each and every day. This means thinking before responding and having a purpose to everything that you do and say. That purpose is to be the best you can be, with these skills underpinning what you do.

We are gradually moving towards a place where there is far greater awareness for the need for these skills. There is more training available to help people develop, schools and colleges are starting to include more experiential learning and help people to be more equipped. But the best person to start this change is you.

Now is the time...

- to take ownership of your life
- to be the best version of yourself that there is and, because of that, have 'The Advantage'.

'Start where you are. Distant fields always look greener, but opportunity lies right where you are.'

Robert Collier

Beyond this text you can visit our free website at www. the-advantage.info where you can find interactive tools and apps, relevant articles and exercises to help you with developing and using these skills day-to-day. You can also find tips, support and access to coaching and training.

For trainers and teachers you can get further support for materials, program design, soft skills and experiential learning activities at www.unimenta.com. Membership is free.

And if you want to write to me directly, I'd love to hear from you! emmasueprince@unimenta.com

Notes

The World We Are Living In

1 www.edweek.org/tsb/articles/2010/10/12/01panel.h04.html

The term '21st-century skills' is generally used to refer to certain core competencies such as collaboration; digital literacy, critical thinking, and problem solving that advocates believe schools need to teach to help students thrive in today's world. In a broader sense, however, the idea of what learning in the 21st century should look like is open to interpretation – and controversy.

Education Week Teacher PD Sourcebook – online discussion, October 2011

2 www.telegraph.co.uk/education/expateducation/9020560/University-to-open-first-UK-campus-in-Thailand.html

Hyslop, L. (January 2012) 'University to open first UK campus in Thailand', *The Telegraph*

3 www.wonkhe.com/2011/06/27/globalisation-where-on-earth-does-he-start/

Hughes, M. (June 2011) 'Globalisation: Where on Earth Does He Start?', Wonkhe – blog for Higher Education sector

4 Autor, D. (April 2010) in 'The polarization of job opportunities in the US Labor Market', Page, S. E. (2008) *The Difference: How the Power of Diversity Creates Better Groups, Firms, Schools and Societies.* Princeton University Press

5 'Economic Views BRICS', www.economics.pwc.com, February 2012

6 Done, A. (2012) *Global Trends: Facing up to a Changing World.* Palgrave Macmillan

7 www.peopleandplanet.net/?lid=25995&section=33&topic=26

'The Ageing World', (January 2008), People & the Planet

8 www.cbi.org.uk/business-issues/education-and-skills/in-focus/education-and-skills-survey/

CBI Education and Skills Survey 2012

9 www.economist.com/node/15640999

'Much to Learn – German's Education System is a Work in Progress', (March 2010), *The Economist*

10 online.wsj.com/article/SB10001424052702303665904577452521454725242.html?mod=WSJ_business_whatsNews

Fuhrmans, V. (June 2012) 'Germany's New Export: Jobs Training', *The Wall Street Journal*

11 www.guardian.co.uk/science/2012/jun/30/self-help-positive-thinking

Wiseman, R. (June 2012) 'Self-Help: forget positive thinking, try positive action', *The Guardian*

12 Economist.com/blogs/Bagehot

'Bagehot's Notebook, Britain's Cheering Gloom', (June 2012), *The Economist*

13 Economist.com/blogs/Bagehot

Chapter 1

1 Buch, K. (2009) 'Adaptability – Leading Through Focused Conversations', The Public Manager

2 www.clarionenterprises.com/assessments-eq.php#eci

3 Barnett, D.; Bauer, A.; Bell, S.; Elliott, N.; Haski, H.; Barkley, E.; Baker, D.; Mackiewicz, K. (22 June 2007) 'Preschool Intervention Scripts: Lessons from 20 years of Research and Practice', *The Journal of Speech-Language Pathology and Applied Behavior Analysis*

4 psychology.about.com/od/crisiscounseling/tp/become-more-resilient.htm

Cherry, K. (2012) *10 Ways to Become More Resilient*

5 www.telegraph.co.uk/health/healthnews/9173552/Learning-another-language-could-protect-against-dementia.html

Adams, S. (March 2012) 'Learning Another Language Could Protect Against Dementia', *The Telegraph*

6 www.trainingzone.co.uk/topic/role-play-real-play/174137

Holmes, S. (May 2012) 'From role play to real play', The Training Zone

7 Jon Wilkerson – www.internationalfunnybusiness.com

8 Calarco, A., Gurvis, J. (2006) *Adaptability : Responding Effectively to Change*. USA: Center for Creative Leadership, p. 12

Chapter 2

1 donaldclarkplanb.blogspot.co.uk/2011/01/huge-study-do-universities-really-teach.html

Clark, D. (2012) 'Do Universities Really Teach Critical Thinking? Apparently Not', Donald Clark Plan B blog

2 cart.critical-thinking.com/critical-thinking-an-interview-part-i

'Critical Thinking' (2012) an interview with Richard C. Wells, BPI's VP of R&D

3 blog.kissmetrics.com/information-explosion/

Kissmetrics – statistics on information explosion, 2012

4 www.criticalthinking.org/pages/dr-linda-elder/819

'The Critical Thinking Community', profile of Dr Linda Elder

5 www.sciencedirect.com/science/article/pii/S0160289610001303

Nusbaum and Silvia (2010) 'Study: Are intelligence and creativity really so different?', *Science Direct*

6 blogs.hbr.org/baldoni/2010/01/how_leaders_should_think_criti.html

Baldoni, J. (January 2010) 'How Leaders Should Think Critically', *Harvard Business Review*

7 www.stanleymilgram.com/milgram.php

Stanley Milgram profile

8 Winner, M.G. (2007) *Thinking About You, Thinking About Me*. Think Social Publishing

9 '*For learners to develop cognitively flexible processing skills and to acquire contentive knowledge structures which can support flexible cognitive processing, flexible learning environments are required which permit the same items of knowledge to be presented and learned in a variety of different ways and for a variety of different purposes (commensurate with their complex and irregular nature).*' Spiro (1996)

10 Winner, M.G. (2005) *Social Behaviour Mapping*. Think Social Publishing

11 www.wired.com/science/discoveries/news/2008/04/smart_software

Madrigal, A. (April 2008) 'Forget Brain Age: Researchers Develop Software That Makes You Smarter'

Chapter 3

1 www.pcmag.com/article2/0,2817,2401474,00.asp

Albanesius, C. (March 2012) 'Twitter's Biz Stone: Embrace Empathy', *PC Magazine*

2 www.washingtonpost.com/national/on-leadership/forget-austerity-or-stimulus-we-need-humanity/2012/03/14/gIQApNSPCS_story.html

Khan, M. (March 2012) 'Forget Austerity or Stimulus, We Need Humanity', *The Washington Post*

3 www.eiconsortium.org/reports/business_case_for_ei.html

Cherniss, C. (1999) 'The Business Case for Emotional Intelligence', Graduate School of Applied and Professional Psychology, Rutgers University

4 www.myiris.com/newsCentre/storyShow.php?fileR=20120711102309 717&dir=2012/07/11

MyIris news site (2010) 'Rising Talent Management Challenges for Rapid Growth', Ernst & Young Survey

5 Page, S.E. (2008) *The Difference: How the Power of Diversity Creates Better Groups, Firms, School and Societies*. Princeton University Press

www.press.princeton.edu

6 www.forbes.com/sites/sap/2011/08/22/ social-media-success-is-just-about-one-thing-empathy/

Wilms, T. (August 2011) 'Social Media Success is Just About One Thing: Empathy', *Forbes Magazine*

7 www.scientificamerican.com/article.cfm?id=what-me-care

Zaki, J. (2012) 'What, Me Care? Young are Less Empathetic', *Scientific American*

8 Singer, T. and Lamm, C. (2009) *The Social Neuroscience of Empathy*. University of Zurich

9 www.livescience.com/220-scientists-read-minds.html

Than, K. (April 2005) 'Scientists Say Everyone Can Read Minds', Live Science

10 www.psychologytoday.com/basics/neuroscience

Neuroscience description in *Psychology Today*

11 www.washingtonpost.com/wpdyn/content/article/2007/05/27/ AR20070527010 html

Vedantam, S. (May 2007) 'If It Feels Good to be Good, It Might Be Only Natural', *The Washington Post*

12 www.psychologytoday.com/basics/altruism

Altruism, Understanding Altruism description from *Psychology Today*

13 www.psychologytoday.com/basics/cognition

Description of Cognition from *Psychology Today*

14 www.danpink.com/whole-new-mind

Pink, D. (2011) *A Whole New Mind*. Marshall Cavendish

15 www.paulekman.com/

Paul Ekman

16 en.wikipedia.org/wiki/Forum_theatre

Definition of Forum theatre

17 www.guardian.co.uk/lifeandstyle/2008/mar/18/healthandwellbeing. features1

Darling, A. (March 2008) 'Mind over Matter', *The Guardian*

18 Langer, E. (1990) *Mindfulness*. Westview Press

19 www.usatoday.com/money/jobcenter/workplace/bruzzese/ story/2012-07-08/meditation-helps-your-work/56071024/1

Bruzzese, A. (October 2012) 'Meditation can keep you more focused at work,' study *USA Today*

20 www.rickhanson.net/

Rick Hanson

21 Neuro-Linguistic Programming:

DEFINITION: A set of models of how communication impacts and is impacted by subjective experience. Techniques are generated from these models by sequencing of various aspects of the models in order to change someone's internal representations. Neurolinguistic programming is concerned with the patterns or programming created by the interactions among the brain, language, and the body, that produce both effective and ineffective behaviour.'

22 www.evancarmichael.com/Leadership/5589/Gandhis-Neurons-The-Practice-of-Empathy.html

[See point 5 of] Carmichael, E., Martinuzzi, B. (2012) 'Gandhi's Neurons: The Practice of Empathy'

Chapter 4

1 Carter, S. L. (1996) *Integrity*. HarperCollins, p. 7

2 'Perspective Leadership Moments', *FBI Law Enforcement Bulletin* (October 2011).

3 www.stephencovey.com/blog/?tag=integrity

Covey, S.R. (October 2008) website, extract from interview: 'Crisis Creates Humility'

4 Fenstermacher, G.D. (22 April 2009) 'How Did We Get Here? The Loss of Integrity in American Life'

An address to the Annual Scholarship Dinner attendees by Professor Emeritus, University of Michigan

Pennsylvania State University, Schuylkill Campus

5 www.brandmovers.com/blog/ so-what-is-monochronic-vs-polychronic-behavior/

Brandmovers Blog (2011) 'What is Monochromic vs Polychronic Behaviour?'

6 www.ame.org/target/articles/1998/07/ best-companies-have-most-integrity

Park, D. and Huge, E. (July 1998) 'The Best Companies Have the Most Integrity', Association for Manufacturing Excellence

Chapter 5

1 www.time.com/time/health/article/0,8599,2074067,00. html#ixzz20QwcyQW1

Sharot, T. (May 2011) 'The Optimism Bias', *Time, Health & Family*

2 en.wikipedia.org/wiki/Law_of_attraction

Description of the Law of Attraction

3 www.oliverburkeman.com/books

4 Berkman, E.T. and Lieberman, M.D. (2010) 'Approaching the bad and avoiding the good: Lateral prefrontal cortical asymmetry distinguishes between action and valence', *Journal of Cognitive Neuroscience*, 22(9), 1970–79

5   Fredrickson, B.L. and Losada, M.F. (2005) 'Positive Affect and the
     Complex Dynamics of Human Flourishing', *American Psychologist*,
     60(7), 678-86.

     Fox. E. (2012) *Rainy Brain Sunny Brain: the New Science of optimism
     and pessimism*. Basic Books.

6   www.guardian.co.uk/science/2011/may/15/
     flourish-science-of-happiness-psychology-review

     Layard, R. (May 2011) 'Flourish: A New Understanding of
     Happiness and Well-Being and How to Achieve Them', *The Guardian*

7   Carroll, P., Sweeny, K., Shepperd, J.A. (2006) 'Forsaking Optimism',
     Review of General Psychology, 10(1), 56–73.

8   Karen Reivich, PHD, University of Pennslyvania, Co-Director Penn
     Resiliency Project: www.ppc.sas.upenn.edu/prpsum.htm

9   www.forbes.com/sites/kevinkruse/2012/06/22/
     employee-engagement-what-and-why/

     Kruse, K. (June 2012) 'What is Employee Engagement', *Forbes
     Magazine*

10 Marshall, G.N., Wortman, C.B., Kusulas, J.W., Hervig, L.K., and
     Vickers, R.R. (1992) 'Distinguishing Optimism From Pessimism:
     Relations to Fundamental Dimensions of Mood and Personality'
     Journal of Personality and Social Psychology, 62(6), 1067–74.

11 Ben-Ze'ev, A. (2000) *The Subtlety of Emotions*. Bradford Books

12 Taylor, S.E. and Brown, J.D. (1994) 'Positive Illusions and Well-Being
     Revisited, Separating Fact from Fiction,' *Psychological Bulletin*, Vol.
     116, No 1, 21–7 (as cited in Taylor and Gollwitzer, 1995).

13 Taylor, S. and Armor, D. (December 1996), 'Positive Illusions and
     Coping with Adversity,' *Journal of Personality*, 64(4), 873–98.

14 Oeetingen, G. (2002) 'The Motivating Function of Thinking About
     the Future: Expectations vs Fantasies,' *Journal of Personality and
     Social Psychology*, 83, 1198–1212.

15 Pham, L. B. (1999) 'From Thought To Action: Effects of Process
     versus Outcome-based Mental Simulations on Performance'
     Personality and Social Psychology Bulletin, 25(2), 250–60.

16 www.hup.harvard.edu/collection.php?cpk=1162

     The work of William James, Harvard University Press

17 www.guardian.co.uk/science/2012/jun/30/
   self-help-positive-thinking?INTCMP=SRCH
   Wiseman, R. (June 2012) 'Self help: Forget positive thinking, try
   positive action', *The Guardian*

18 www.clarku.edu/faculty/jlaird/Publications.htm
   About James Laird – research into the perception of self

19 Seligman, M. *Learned Optimism: How to Change Your Mind and
   Your Life.* Vintage Books USA.

20 www.forbes.com/2009/01/15/self-help-industry-ent-sales-cx_
   ml_0115selfhelp.html

Chapter 6

1 Covey, S.R. (2004) *The 7 Habits of Highly Effective People: Personal
   Workbook.* Simon & Schuster

2 www.lifehack.org/articles/productivity/are-you-proactive-or-reactive.
   html

3 Grant, A.M. and Ashford, S.J. (2008) 'The dynamics of proactivity at
   work,' *Research in Organizational Behaviour*, 28, 3–34.

4 Bindl, U. and Parker, S. (2010) 'Proactive Work Behaviour: Forward-
   Thinking and Change-Oriented Action in Organizations,' Institute of
   Work Psychology, University of Sheffield

5 *Journal of Leadership and Organisational Studies* (August 2009)

6 www.linkedin.com

7 Crant, M. (July 1996) 'The proactive personality scale as a predictor
   of entrepreneurial intentions' *Journal of Small Business Management*,
   34(3) 42, 2 charts.

8 Dweck, C.S. (1999) *Self-Theories: Their Role in Motivation, Personality,
   and Development.* The Psychology Press.

9 Steel, P. (2011) *The Procrastination Equation: How to Stop Putting
   Things Off and Start Getting More Done.* Pearson Education.

10 Viktor Emil Frankl, MD, PhD was an Austrian neurologist and
   psychiatrist as well as a Holocaust survivor. Frankl was the founder
   of logotherapy, which is a form of existential analysis, the 'Third
   Viennese School of Psychotherapy.'

11 Kirby, E.G., Kirby, S.L., Lewis, M.A. (July 2002) 'A Study of the
   Effectiveness of Training Proactive Thinking,' *Journal of Applied Social
   Psychology*, 32(7), 1538–49, Southwest Texas State University.

Chapter 7

1 Kelly, R. (2005) *'innate psychological human immune capacity'* in 'Developing resilience', Affinity Health at Work (2011)

2 Greef (2002) *'a multi-faceted process from which people draw and learn from the best they can find in their environment, which can include family, school or the community'* in 'Developing resilience', Affinity Health at Work (2011)

3 Richardson (2002) *'categories that promote resilience, namely individual dispositional attributes, family support and cohesion and external support systems'* in 'Developing resilience', Affinity Health at Work (2011)

4 Jessica Pryce-Jones, CEO of iOPener, a human asset management consultancy and author of *Happiness at Work*

5 Hinsliff, G. (2012) *'Half a Wife', The Working Family's Guide to Getting a Life Back*. Chatto & Windus

6 Hughes, D. and Sobczak, K. (2011) 'Thriving Through Change: Developing Leadership Resilience', a & dc

7 www.ted.com/pages/about

About TED

8 www.ted.com/talks/lang/en/richard_st_john_s_8_secrets_of_success. html

TED talk, Richard St John – '8 Secrets of Success'

9 www.ppc.sas.upenn.edu/prpsum.htm

University of Pennsylvania, Positive Psychology Center

10 The curriculum teaches cognitive-behavioural and social problem-solving skills and is based in part on cognitive-behavioural theories of depression by Aaron Beck, Albert Ellis and Martin Seligman (Abramson, Seligman, & Teasdale, 1978; Beck, 1967, 1976; Ellis, 1962). Central to PRP is Ellis' Adversity-Consequences-Beliefs (ABC) model, the notion that our beliefs about events mediate their impact on our emotions and behaviour.

11 SIT is a form of cognitive restructuring as it is a method of changing an individual's thinking patterns about themselves and their lives. The aim is to change their emotional responses and their behaviour, ideally before the individual becomes very anxious or depressed as a result of stress.

'Stress Innoculation Training: A preventative and treatment approach.' Dr Donald Meichenbaum, chapter in Lehrer, P. M., Woolfolk, R. L. and Sime, W. S., (2007) *Principles and Practice of Stress Management* (3rd edition), Guilford Press..

12 Duckworth, A.L., Peterson, C., Matthews, M.D. and Kelly, D.R. (2006) 'Grit, perseverance and passion for long-term goals,' *Journal of Personality and Social Psychology*, 92(6), 1087–101.

Index